Robert Altman Hollywood Survivor

Robert Altman

Hollywood Survivor

Daniel O'Brien

B. T. Batsford Ltd. London

First published 1995

© Daniel O'Brien 1995

All rights reserved. No part of this
publication may be reproduced, in any
form or by any means, without permission
from the Publisher

Typeset by Goodfellow & Egan

and printed in Great Britain by
Biddles, Guildford

Published by

B.T. Batsford Ltd
4 Fitzhardinge Street
London W1H 0AH

A CIP catalogue record for this book is
available from the British Library

ISBN 0 7134 7481 5

Frontispiece: Robert Altman

Contents

Acknowledgements

My thanks to the following for offering their thoughts on both Robert Altman and this book: Gary Kramer (who also tracked down invaluable Altman material), Justin O'Brien, Mark Lonsdale and my agent David O'Leary. Thanks also to Timothy Auger and Richard Reynolds at B.T. Batsford Ltd, Sue Donkin at Channel Four, Viacom and Artificial Eye.

ILLUSTRATIONS: *Short Cuts* stills courtesy of Artificial Eye Film Co. All other stills supplied by the British Film Institute Stills, Posters and Designs department. All the photographs were originally issued for publicity or promotion by United Artists (*The Delinquents*; *The Long Goodbye*; *Thieves Like Us*; *Buffalo Bill and the Indians*), Warner Bros. (*Countdown*; *McCabe and Mrs Miller*), Commonwealth International (*That Cold Day in the Park*), Twentieth Century Fox (*M*A*S*H*; *Three Women*; *A Wedding*; *Quintet*; *A Perfect Couple*; *Health*), Metro Goldwyn Mayer (*Brewster McCloud*), Hemdale/Columbia (*Images*), Columbia (*California Split*), Paramount (*Nashville*; *Popeye*), Sandcastle 5/Viacom (*Come Back to the Five and Dime, Jimmy Dean, Jimmy Dean*), Rank Film Distributors (*Streamers*), MGM/UA (*O.C. and Stiggs*), Sandcastle 5 (*Secret Honor*), The Cannon Group (*Fool for Love*), New World Pictures (*Beyond Therapy*), Central Films/Blue Dolphin Films (*Vincent and Theo*), Spelling Films International/Guild Film Distribution (*The Player*) and Artificial Eye Film Co (*Short Cuts*).

1

Introduction

In the final sequence of *McCabe and Mrs Miller* (1971), John McCabe, gambler, businessman and romantic dreamer, is stalked through the snow-covered streets of a small western town. His pursuers are three gunmen hired by a large mining company to dispose of anyone who stands in the way of their business operations. As the snow falls ever thicker, McCabe takes on the killers one by one, shooting them all dead, but is himself mortally wounded. Collapsing in the snow, his body is steadily covered by the blizzard, eventually disappearing from view altogether. Unwitnessed by any of the townsfolk, his act of reckless courage in the face of an unbeatable enemy will remain forever a secret.

Up until the success of *The Player* (1992), Robert Altman, director, producer and writer, must have felt more than a passing empathy with John McCabe. One of the most talented and individual American film-makers, Altman's preference for offbeat characters, experimental techniques and improvisation, combined with his general disregard for the clichés of mainstream cinema, has produced a succession of outstanding films. At the same time, the limited box-office returns generated by these films and his own uncompromising attitude have come close to killing his career. After a decade largely confined to low-budget, independently-produced filmed plays, Altman's return to prominence with *The Player*, while not exactly a return from the celluloid grave, has regained him his status as a major creative force in the cinema. It is entirely appropriate that the film is a sharp satire on contemporary Hollywood, a world with which Altman has enjoyed an unorthodox and often tortuous relationship.

Though best known for his 1970 success, *M*A*S*H*, Altman's film career dates back as far as the late forties, when, barely in his twenties, he sought employment at the major Hollywood studios as a writer and actor. Little came of this (some work, not always credited, on original stories and a short-term contract as an extra) and nearly a decade passed before he was given another chance to break into feature films. Shot on location in Altman's home town of Kansas City, Missouri, *The Delinquents* (1957), which he produced, wrote and directed, was a low-budget 'teenage angst' drama in the *Rebel Without a Cause* tradition. This was followed, appropriately, by *The James Dean Story* (1957), an interesting, though uneven feature-length documentary on which Altman worked as co-director and producer. Both films were picked up for distribution by major studios (United Artists and Warner Brothers respectively) but did not lead to any offers of work in Hollywood. Altman abandoned the cinema for television, where for the next decade he worked as a director (and occasional writer) of series episodes and plays.

Established as a successful, if controversial television director (his penchant for rewriting scripts incurred the wrath of more than one executive producer), Altman spent much of the sixties attempting to break back into feature films. After a number of false starts and a lot of grief, he was hired by Warner Brothers to direct *Countdown* (1968), a well-made, if instantly dated piece of science fiction about the American–Soviet space race. Atypical of his later work, *Countdown* is mainly notable for its accomplished leading performances (early starring roles for James Caan and Robert Duvall) and an ambivalent attitude towards the 'heroics' of space flight.

Altman's next film, *That Cold Day in the Park* (1969), proved rather more distinctive. A psychological drama concerning an eccentric, sexually-repressed spinster who first befriends, then imprisons a lonely young man, it revealed the director's interest in character studies of bizarre individuals. The film also exhibited the first real traces of what was to develop into Altman's unique film-making style. Variously described as 'fly-on-the-wall', 'eavesdropping' and 'mock realism', this technique employs such devices as overlapping sound (background noise and conversation compete with the main thread of dialogue for the audience's attention) and an inquisitive, probing camera which endlessly explores the narrative space of the film, zooming past (and cutting away from) the main characters to linger on some background figure or object. The effect of this method is what Robert Kolker, in *A Cinema of Loneliness*, terms a 'decentralisation' of space (both visual and aural). Events on the edge of the frame can be as interesting or important as the action (or inaction) in the middle. If *That Cold Day in the Park* marked the arrival of a notable talent, Altman's next project showed that his style could be profitable.

M*A*S*H proved to be Altman's breakthrough film. A wild black comedy (ironic black humour, sometimes too black for audience tastes, was to become an Altman trademark) set during the Korean War, it centred on a

Popeye – Popeye (Robin Williams) and Oxblood Oxheart (Peter Bray)

group of surgeons stationed at a mobile army hospital. Plot was subordinated to characterization and atmosphere, giving plenty of opportunity to leads Donald Sutherland and Elliott Gould, both of whom became stars as a result. Working with the ultra-wide Panavision format (the major successor to Cinemascope), Altman was able to further develop his visual style (though *Countdown* was filmed in the same format, he'd been given little opportunity to experiment with it) and the script enabled him to play with various themes (anarchy, camaraderie, misogyny, racism, leadership) which were to recur in much of his later work. A big commercial success, *M*A*S*H* secured Altman's reputation and gave him the chance to make the films he wanted in collaboration with major studios.

Throughout the first half of the seventies, Altman brought his unique style to a variety of genres, including the western (*McCabe and Mrs Miller* (1971)), the psychological drama (*Images* (1972)), the private eye drama (*The Long Goodbye* (1973)) and the crime film (*Thieves Like Us* (1974)). Working with a more or less established team of collaborators, both behind and in front of the camera (though there were inevitable changes in personnel over the years), he followed a fixed pattern of production: medium budgets (always under $5 million), location shooting (away from studio interference), offbeat casting (often using unknown actors such as Shelley Duvall and Keith Carradine) and a relaxed atmosphere (likened by biographer Patrick McGilligan to a 'family' group with Altman as the benevolent father figure). Actors would be encouraged to contribute ideas for their characters and improvise dialogue (though it would end up on the cutting room floor if it didn't add to the overall film). Each member of the production team would be invited to screenings of the day's 'rushes' (the footage shot and printed during one day's filming) and asked for comments and constructive criticism. Altman's most ambitious film from this period is *Nashville* (1975), an epic, multi-character drama concerning a disparate group of country, folk and gospel singers and the attempts of an unscrupulous political adviser to recruit them for his candidate's rally. Regarded by many as its director's greatest achievement, *Nashville* has become a milestone in the history of American cinema.

This period of Altman's career is generally regarded as his most fruitful, but the problems that later cast him into the film-makers' wilderness were already apparent. Prominent among these was his relationship with the big studios, which ranged from wariness to outright hostility. These studios, such as Twentieth Century Fox (which produced *M*A*S*H*), Metro Goldwyn Mayer, United Artists and Columbia, had been through a traumatic period of box-office disasters and corporate takeovers during the late sixties and early seventies and had little time for a director who demanded artistic freedom (Altman produced many of his films through his own company, Lion's Gate) without offering a commercial hit in return. The promise of another *M*A*S*H* kept studios interested but the subsequent films rarely did more than recover their costs. Altman retaliated by accusing the studio executives of losing faith in his work and giving the films inadequate distribution. The result was a series of production deals with six different companies in as many years. By way of compensation, Altman enjoyed a large measure of critical acclaim, both at home and abroad, and *Nashville* received both favourable reviews and solid commercial success. His reputation with actors also secured him the services of stars such as Warren Beatty, Julie Christie, Susannah York and Paul Newman (though he seldom felt the need to employ box-office names).

The second half of the decade should, in theory, have given Altman a little more stability as, after the flop of *Buffalo Bill and the Indians* (1976), he secured a multi-picture deal with Twentieth Century Fox. The first of these, *Three Women* (1977), proved to be one of his finest films, though its defiantly uncommercial approach doomed it to a negligible 'arthouse' release. The subsequent films, *A Wedding* (1978), *Quintet* (1979), *A Perfect Couple* (1979) and *Health* (1980), were less esoteric but several of them exhibited a certain patchiness in both style and content. Critical response became gradually more hostile, Fox's distribution division showed little inclination to market the films and the already minimal box-office receipts dried up entirely. Altman was increasingly looked on as a burned-out talent, unable to operate under the Hollywood rules and too ready to badmouth those he felt had let him down (widespread rumours of drug and alcohol abuse didn't help).

To the surprise of many, in 1979 Altman was given the chance to re-establish himself as a commercial director when Robert Evans, a producer based at Paramount, hired him to direct *Popeye* (1980), a live-action version of the famous comic strip and cartoon series. Co-financed by the Walt Disney Company, the film marked the motion picture debut of television star and stand-up comedian Robin Williams in the title role, with Altman regular Shelley Duvall as Olive Oyl. A gentle musical comedy, aimed at a family audience, *Popeye* seemed an unlikely vehicle for the director's idiosyncratic style. In fact, it turned out to be one of Altman's best films, his offbeat treatment of story and characters capturing perfectly the slightly bizarre atmosphere of the original cartoons. Unfortunately, Altman's already tarnished reputation, along with rumours of trouble on the *Popeye* production and budget over-runs, led to disparaging pre-release publicity. Released to mixed, often uncomprehending reviews, *Popeye* was a box-office disappointment and Altman's career slumped to its lowest point since his mid-sixties struggles.

Dropped by the big studios, Altman spent most of the eighties directing

Robert Altman directing *California Split*

film versions of stage plays, including *Come Back to the Five and Dime, Jimmy Dean, Jimmy Dean* (1982), which he had also directed in the theatre, *Streamers* (1983), *Secret Honor* (1984) and *Fool for Love* (1985). Respectfully received (by and large) and boasting gifted players (among them Sandy Dennis, Cher, Matthew Modine and Harry Dean Stanton), these films provided ample evidence that Altman's talent had not deserted him but had a very limited audience appeal. An attempt at a mainstream comeback, the National Lampoon-inspired *O.C. and Stiggs* (filmed in 1983), proved a disaster and *Beyond Therapy* (1987), an opened-out version of a play about 'zany' psychiatrists and their patients, stands as Altman's worst film to date. Successful work for cable television, notably the political satire *Tanner '88* (1988), served to bolster his reputation a little until the French-British co-production *Vincent and Theo* (1990) gave Altman the chance to move away from the confines of filmed theatre and resurrect his moribund film career.

A moving, if slightly impersonal account of the troubled relationship between the artist Van Gogh and his art dealer brother, *Vincent and Theo* compares with the best of Altman's early seventies work. Praised by critics as a return to form, the film brought the director back into the public eye without giving him the commercial muscle necessary to impress the American studios. Fortunately, Altman's success with *The Player* has restored him to the ranks of 'bankable' directors. His subsequent film, *Short Cuts* (1993), a large-scale adaptation of several stories by Raymond Carver, has been compared to *Nashville* and won the Golden Lion Best Film Award at the 1993 Venice Film Festival.

Robert Altman has been criticized more than once for self-indulgence and laziness. His desire to be different is said to result in films with wandering storylines, incomprehensible characters (accentuated by inaudible soundtracks) and a lack of pace which quickly slides into tedium. His trademark use of the slow zoom is looked on by more traditionally-minded filmmakers as simply the mark of a careless, unimaginative director. His preference for shooting only a few takes of a scene (to obtain what he regards as more spontaneous and realistic performances) antagonizes actors used to being given time to develop their characters (Altman has little interest in this approach, arguing that 'casting is ninety-per-cent of the creative work').

Yet in Altman's best work (*Nashville* excepted), this apparently casual style is as deceptive as his characters' seeming passiveness and incompetence. The doctors in *M*A*S*H* may spend all their free time playing practical jokes, flouting authority and getting drunk, but this is shown to be a legitimate response to the horrendous bloodshed they are faced with daily. They demonstrate their responsibility and skill in the operating theatre. In

The Long Goodbye, Elliott Gould's Philip Marlowe is pushed around by gangsters and police alike, but proves his abilities as a private eye by solving a vicious murder case. When he discovers that the killer is a supposed friend who tricked him into helping him escape justice, Marlowe tracks the man down and shoots him dead. There is plenty of drama in the lives of Altman's major protagonists, but he is always equally concerned with the nature of these lives and the worlds they inhabit. The narratives of his fully-realized works are as carefully developed as the characterizations, each element contributing to the film as a whole. The multiple strands of storyline in *Nashville*, for example, are expertly interwoven, coming neatly together for the downbeat finale.

If Altman is to be criticized, it is for an occasional tendency to undermine his abilities as a director through a lack of self-discipline. Several films collapse under a mass of offbeat characters, observation and detail incorporated with no thought as to their place in the overall structure. Robert Altman has yet to make a boring film (though some would argue that *Quintet*, a bizarre science fiction fantasy, comes fairly close) but a number leave an exasperating sense of opportunities missed in pursuit of the easy laugh or the weird aside. His preference for outlandish behaviour can also result in an unrelenting (and unilluminating) emphasis on thinly-sketched characters who seem merely foolish, neurotic and arrogant.

While this book contains biographical details, it is not intended as a comprehensive account of Robert Altman's life, rather a chronological account of his remarkable career in feature films from 1947 onwards. After a lengthy, often frustrating apprenticeship in industrial films, second features and networked television, Altman emerged during the early seventies as one of the cinema's foremost talents. Many of his films, such as *M*A*S*H*, *McCabe and Mrs Miller*, *The Long Goodbye* and *Nashville*, are now regarded as 'modern classics'. Virtually unknown up until the age of forty-five, written off at fifty-five and now on a new creative wave as he reaches his seventieth year, Robert Altman is both a great film-maker and a great survivor.

Shelley Duvall on the set of *McCabe and Mrs Miller*

2

Delinquents and Whirlybirds

Born in Kansas City in 1925 to prosperous, upper-middle-class parents, Robert Bernard Altman's first experiences of the cinema included the usual family outings, and screenings at his school on special occasions. The school, an enlightened Catholic establishment, also organized day trips to the local cinemas when the current attractions were felt to be of particular merit. (This religious side of Altman's upbringing has led several critics to root out the 'classic' Catholic themes in his films: guilt, fatalism, death-fixation, redemption, leadership and an ambivalent treatment of women. While several of these elements do recur in the director's work, they are hardly exclusive to this one Christian denomination. Nor is it particularly helpful to reduce the multifarious influences on Altman's thematic pre-occupations to one aspect of his childhood.) None of Altman's immediate family had any connections to the film business (his father, Bernard Clement Altman, was an insurance salesman), though an aunt, Pauline Altman Walsh, wrote popular tunes, several of which ended up in films (such as 'Christmas Story', sung by Doris Day in *On Moonlight Bay* (1951)).

His first brush with the world of Hollywood came in 1945 during his air force training (Altman flew a number of bombing missions as a co-pilot during World War II) at a base near Los Angeles, California, home of the film industry. Following his military service, Altman drifted through a number of occupations (including a short stint in insurance) before deciding to become a film actor. In 1946 he married his first wife, LaVonne Elmer. Their short-lived union produced a daughter (Christine, born 1947) before the couple's separation and eventual divorce in the early fifties.

An agent secured a short-term contract for Altman at Twentieth Century Fox, but his mid-western accent proved a handicap to obtaining work. Probably the highlight of this brief stage in his career was on loan-out as an extra to producer Samuel Goldwyn for an appearance in *The Secret Life of*

Walter Mitty (1947), a vehicle for top box-office star Danny Kaye.

Altman enjoyed a slight upturn in his Hollywood fortunes when he met George W. George, an assistant director who happened to be a tenant of his parents (at this time residing in Malibu). Together they wrote the original story for *Bodyguard* (1948), a modest *film noir* directed by Richard Fleischer for RKO (a company jointly founded by the Radio Corporation of America and the Keith-Orpheum cinema circuit). Altman then wrote (uncredited) the original story for *Christmas Eve* (1947), a forgettable melodrama made by independent producer Benedict Bogeaus for United Artists, starring George Raft and Randolph Scott (neither at the peak of their careers). While it would be a mistake to attach any great significance to these minor efforts, it is worth remembering that, having obtained his first screen credit, Altman was to labour for over twenty years before finally achieving Hollywood recognition with *M*°*A*°*S*°*H*.

Unfortunately, Altman's minor inroads into the film industry quickly came to a dead end. The late forties was not a good time for would-be scriptwriters. The immediate post-war period had seen an alarming decline in cinema attendances (with the accompanying fall in revenue for the studios), a bad situation which the rapidly-growing popularity of television could only make worse. Added to this was the unstable climate within the industry. The House of Un-American Activities Committee (HUAC), dedicated to rooting out 'communist subversion' in American society, had turned its attention to Hollywood, wrecking a number of careers and creating an overall feeling of wariness. Altman could not obtain any more work and by the end of the decade he had returned in Kansas City.

Back home, Altman did not abandon film-making, but found employment with the Calvin Company, a leading producer of industrial films, commercials, government films, documentaries and educational films. It was here that he learned the basic skills of film production: scripting, directing, photography, sound, editing, processing and budgeting. As McGilligan notes, though Altman was confined to very tight budgets and production schedules, he was already showing his inclination to experiment with film technology, most noticeably in his use of an overlapping soundtrack. This irritated both his Calvin employers and clients, who much preferred clarity as opposed to atmosphere, and Altman was reputedly fired several times over antagonizing customers with his film-making style.

1950 also saw a brief return (of sorts) to feature films for Altman, when he was offered the chance to co-write a country-and-western musical comedy, *Corn's-A-Poppin'* (1951). Directed by Robert Woodburn for Kansas-based producer Elmer Rhoden Jr. (Elmer Rhoden Sr. owned a chain of cinemas across the mid-west), the film was intended as a spoof of backstage musicals. Unseen since its limited original release (according to

McGilligan, the ownership rights are in dispute), *Corn's-A-Poppin'* is reputedly dreadful, though its star, Jerry Wallace, later achieved fame (of a kind) by writing the title song for the sixties television series *Flipper*.

Throughout the early fifties, Altman continued to turn out films for Calvin (around 60 in all), picking up a number of industry awards for his work. He also branched out into television, co-producing and directing (with Robert Woodburn) *Pulse of the City* (1953), a *Dragnet*-inspired cop show, for a local network. Altman was still hoping for another chance to break into Hollywood and in 1955 *Corn's-A-Poppin'* producer Elmer Rhoden Jr. hired him to write and direct a feature film about juvenile delinquency.

Shot on a low budget (between $45,000 and $63,000 with Altman receiving $3,000 for his services) in under three weeks, *The Delinquents* was nevertheless regarded by Altman as a real chance to establish his credentials as a film-maker. The casting for the leads was done in Hollywood and included the actors Peter Miller (who had recently appeared in *The Blackboard Jungle* (1955), one of the first 'dangerous youth' melodramas) and Tom Laughlin (later to achieve national celebrity as the writer/director/star of *Billy Jack* (1971) and its sequels). Altman also insisted on a clause in his contract stating that all the editing and post-production on *The Delinquents* would be done in Hollywood using professional facilities.

The supporting cast was assembled from the ranks of the Calvin Company and the local Jewish Community Center Theatre, while many Kansas City residents appeared as extras (including the local police as themselves). Altman also recruited from his own family, casting his second wife Lotus Corelli (their marriage, in 1954, lasted three years) and his daughter Christine. The filming went relatively smoothly, the only real problems arising from Altman's clashes with leading man Tom Laughlin. An actor with 'method' pretensions (i.e. living his role), Laughlin would delay the shooting of a particular scene by refusing to act until he felt complete empathy with his character. He responded to Altman's remonstrations by threatening to quit *The Delinquents* halfway through production.

Shot in a style described as varying between *cinéma vérité* and self-conscious artiness, *The Delinquents* is a moderately interesting, if unexceptional exploitation film which does not really relate to its creator's later career. The script, written by Altman in less than a week, is a standard mixture of misunderstood teenagers, wild parties, gang violence (quite strong for the period) and petty crime with the inevitable 'society is to blame' coda. Overly melodramatic, and saddled with a very mannered performance by Laughlin, the film's main asset is its striking black and white photography (by Charles Paddock, another Calvin employee), modelled on the style of John Huston's *The Asphalt Jungle* (1950). United Artists were sufficiently impressed by *The Delinquents* to pick up the distribution rights for $150,000. After adding a slightly risible narration, warning concerned parents of the dangers of juvenile delinquency, they released the film in March 1957.

Altman did not wait for the opening of *The Delinquents* before making another attempt to get a foothold in Hollywood. Returning to California in 1956, he spent a year going round the party circuit, trying to make contacts and find work. Nothing came of these efforts (McGilligan suggests that Altman simply did not have the right credentials for employment in Los Angeles) and Altman was back in Kansas when he had the idea of making a film about the recently deceased teen idol, James Dean.

Co-produced and co-directed with his old writing partner, George W. George, *The James Dean Story* began life as a series of interviews (with relatives, friends and colleagues of Dean) and linking footage shot by Altman and fellow Calvin veteran Louis Lombardo. In need of a script, George and

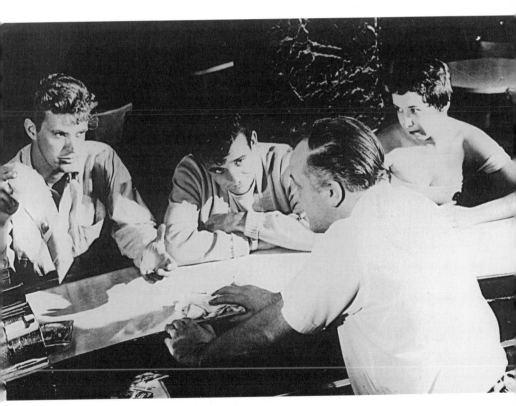

The Delinquents

Altman hired Hollywood writer Stewart Stern, co-author of *Rebel Without a Cause* (1955) and a friend of James Dean. Warner Brothers bought the uncompleted film for distribution, added some James Dean footage of their own (not to mention a theme song, 'Let Me Be Loved') and hired actor Martin Gabel to provide the narration.

Altman contributed some impressive sequences to *The James Dean Story*, notably a dramatic reconstruction of the fatal car crash, but it is doubtful he felt much empathy with the film's attitude to its subject, which borders on hagiography. Twenty-five years later, *Come Back to the Five and Dime, Jimmy Dean, Jimmy Dean* would take a less than flattering look at the legacy left behind by the James Dean phenomenon. That said, the film proved significant for Altman in at least one respect, for during its production he was introduced to the zoom lens (then a fairly new gadget), a device which was to become an integral part of his film-making style.

The release of *The Delinquents* did not result in any offers of film work coming Altman's way, but it was seen and admired by Alfred Hitchcock, who recommended the director to Joan Harrison, producer of his hit television programme *Alfred Hitchcock Presents*, a series of twist-in-the-tail mini-thrillers introduced (and occasionally directed) by the celebrated 'Master of Suspense'. Already two seasons old, *Alfred Hitchcock Presents* was a prestige show, employing top writers (such as Ray Bradbury and Roald Dahl) and featuring a number of actors (Steve McQueen, Burt Reynolds, Robert Redford) and directors (William Friedkin, Sidney Pollack) who would go on to bigger things.

Altman joined the production team of *Alfred Hitchock Presents* during the third series, directing two episodes: *The Young One* (1957), starring Carol Lynley, and *Together* (1958), with Joseph Cotten. Then things went wrong in a major fashion, though the exact reasons are not clear. Altman claims that he was allotted a third script for the show, which he rejected on the grounds of poor quality and advised Harrison not to use at all. It transpired that Harrison had developed this particular script herself and so, unsurprisingly, Altman was not offered any more work on *Alfred Hitchcock Presents*.

The late Joan Harrison disputed this version of events, mainly on the basis that she did not write any of the scripts for the third season of the show. McGilligan suggests that Altman's fall from grace stemmed from his work on another Hitchcock television series, *Suspicion* (1958). Shooting some second unit footage on location in New York, Altman became deeply irritated by the practices of the local union bosses and gave an interview to *Variety* (the film industry's weekly trade journal), criticizing the Teamsters Union for, among other things, blackmailing him into employing union men and equipment he did not need (the alternative being a shutdown in production). Though Altman was by no means alone in his dislike of such dealings, the received wisdom was not to complain, and his public outburst effectively terminated his employment on the Hitchcock shows. This antagonism between Altman and the various film industry unions was to resurface at regular intervals throughout his career.

Altman quickly found employment at the decidedly less prestigious Desilu studio, a company owned by the wife and husband team of Lucille Ball and Desi Arnaz, directing episodes of *The Whirlybirds* (1957–8). Though hardly a classic of the small screen, this particular show is of interest for a number of reasons (one being the similarity between the title sequence and that later used in *M*A*S*H*). The basic format, a couple of for-hire helicopter pilots involved in daring rescues and law enforcement, meant a lot of location shooting, rare at the time for a low-budget show churned out at a rate of two-and-a-half episodes a week. Free from producer interference, Altman was permitted to experiment a little (while remaining within budget, of course). He claims that it was while working on this and later series that he began to develop some of the techniques that would reappear (in rather more refined form) in his films. If he finished a particular episode before two o'clock in the afternoon, Altman and his crew were contractually obliged to start work on the next one. In order to prolong filming till after the deadline, Altman began devising more complicated set-ups, such as reflection shots. Similarly, rather than adhere to scripts that were often of dubious quality, he preferred to let his actors change their lines or to rewrite himself. Altman also tended not to block out an actor's movements during the shooting of a particular scene, but to let them move more freely. So long as the actors were kept in frame (which, as McGilligan notes, led to the unheard of practice of moving the camera while dialogue was being spoken) the producers stayed happy. During his employment at Desilu, Altman met his third wife-to-be, Kathryn Reed, a former model turned film and television extra.

The Whirlybirds was followed by two more shows for Desilu, *US Marshall* (1958) and *The Troubleshooters* (1959), another location-oriented series which Altman devised himself. Altman also landed a job directing episodes of *The Millionaire* (1958–9) for executive producer Don Fedderson. Fedderson respected Altman's talents, but was rather less tolerant than the Desilu producers of his penchant for changing scripts (usually the endings). While actors and technicians grew to appreciate Altman's inventiveness and desire to experiment, production executives were seldom enthusiastic.

1959 saw a return to upmarket television for Altman, when he was hired by Warner Brothers. Warner's television division produced shows for the

ABC network, winning high ratings, favourable reviews and a handful of awards. Altman was set to work on single episodes of *Hawaiian Eye* (1959), *Lawman* (1959), *Surfside Six* (1960–1) and *Maverick* (1960), with a young(ish) Roger Moore, among others. Operating under close supervision and tight schedules, he had little opportunity to function as much more than a hired hand, though occasional writing assignments came his way. Simultaneous to his Warner stint, Altman found work (as a director only) on the second season of the popular western series *Bonanza* (1960–1), whose creator/producer David Dortort was later to comment that he seemed increasingly dissatisfied with the limitations of the television series format.

Still determined to get a feature film off the ground, Altman's employment at Warner Television seemed to be leading nowhere until, in 1961, the studio offered him the chance to direct *The Force*, a no-nonsense, shoot-'em-up action movie. The storyline involved the Canadian Mounted Police chasing after drug smugglers. Suitable locations were found in Vancouver and a budget approved before Warner abandoned the project, citing the costs of location shooting and the uncertainties attached to using a first-time director (presumably *The Delinquents* did not count).

Altman departed for Twentieth Century Fox Television, where he directed several instalments of *Bus Stop* (1961), a series of self-contained dramas. One of his episodes, *A Lion Walks Among Us*, featured clean-cut singing star Fabian Forte Bonaparte as a psychotic murderer and provoked a great deal of controversy at a period when television violence was regarded as a cause for public concern. Though cut before transmission, *A Lion Walks Among Us* was condemned for its brutality. Sponsors withdrew their adverts from its broadcast slot and a number of Fox-affiliated stations refused to screen it at all. Altman appears to have emerged from the whole business unscathed, receiving praise from within the industry for his taut direction of the dark melodrama.

For all his dislike of the television straitjacket, Altman was making progress up the industry ladder. On ABC's *Combat* (1962–3), his last major series, he acted as both director and producer and even had a say in the casting. An unusually downbeat World War II drama, *Combat* built up a high reputation under Altman's guidance (he directed nearly half of the first season's 32 episodes). One episode, *The Volunteer*, was screened at the Venice Film Festival. The regular cast, headed by Vic Morrow, featured several future film collaborators (Michael Murphy, Bob Fortier) and the impressive list of guest stars included Charles Bronson, Lee Marvin, John Cassavetes, Dennis Hopper, James Caan and Robert Duvall. Ultimately, however, *Combat* proved to be a bitter experience for Altman. After a dispute with executive producer Selig Seligman (one bone of contention undoubtedly being his unauthorized script rewrites), he left the series. Seligman disliked Altman's approach, regarding his episodes as unrelentingly grim. *Combat* ran for several more years but its driving force headed off for Universal.

Looked at from a short-term perspective, Altman's brief stint as a producer/director for Universal's *Kraft Theater* (1963), sponsored by the famed cheese manufacturer, was fairly disastrous. Having just quarrelled with his executive producer at ABC, he soon found himself in the same predicament with Roy Huggins, Seligman's opposite number at Universal. Huggins would not tolerate Altman's tendency to alter scripts (changing the endings, in Huggins' words, from 'a bang to a whimper'). Deeply fed up, Altman gave another interview to *Variety*, this time attacking executive producers. After this, his departure from Universal was merely a matter of time.

Against this, it should be noted that Altman's employment under Huggins gave him a chance to meet up again with Lou Lombardo, then working as an assistant editor for Universal. He also became acquainted with three more film collaborators-to-be: editor Danford B. Greene, line producer Robert Eggenweiler and composer John Williams (later to achieve fame and fortune with his scores for *Jaws* (1975), *Star Wars* (1977), *Superman* (1978), *Raiders of the Lost Ark* (1981), and *E.T.* (1982), among many others). All four worked on Altman's last assignment for Universal, which (somewhat ironically) was a film, albeit of the 'tv movie' variety.

Once Upon a Savage Night (1964), a thriller about the pursuit of a serial killer known only as 'Georgie Porgie' (who no doubt kissed the girls and made them die), was based on a book, *Killer on the Turnpike*, by William P. McGivern. Working from a screenplay by Donald Moessinger, Altman shot the film on location and in colour, using a new kind of high-speed film stock (Kodak Ektachrome) which permitted shooting under very low light conditions. Lurid and fairly gruesome, *Once Upon a Savage Night* may not constitute great art, but it provided a spectacular note on which to exit from Universal. Padded with out-takes and retitled *Nightmare in Chicago*, the film was later given a limited drive-in release as the lower half of a double bill. Altman had finally made a return to the cinema, though in a roundabout, back-door way he could scarcely have intended.

3

Countdown to M*A*S*H

Having exited from Universal in 1963 (to the relief of all concerned), Altman now made a determined attempt to break out of television for good and get a feature film into production. In partnership with producer Ray Wagner, another former Universal employee, he began to develop a number of scripts, the most promising of which were *Petulia*, an offbeat romance based on an unpublished novel, *Me and the Arch-Kook Petulia*, by John Haase, and *Death, Where is Thy Sting?*, a black comedy about World War I flyers. To further their ambitions, Altman and Wagner secured the services of respected Hollywood agent (and occasional producer) George Litto. Though initially wary of Altman, whose 'maverick' reputation had already made him a controversial industry figure (the director made little attempt to play down his 'bad boy' image, citing veteran Hollywood rebel/exile Orson Welles as his role model), Litto was to play a vital role in developing the film-maker's career over the next decade.

Death, Where is Thy Sting? (later retitled *The Chicken and the Hawk*) originated as an idea for yet another television series (at one point Litto sold the concept to Screen Gems) but quickly became upgraded to a big budget action film. Brian McKay, a friend of Altman's wife Kathryn, worked on the storyline, which was to be handed over to Roald Dahl for tranformation into a screenplay. At the same time, writer Barbara Turner (wife of *Combat* star Vic Morrow) put together the script for *Petulia*. Altman contributed ideas to both projects, though whether he did any actual writing himself is disputed. Unsympathetic observers have claimed that Altman's status as a writer is questionable; for all his ability to produce original ideas for films, he finds the process of developing them into a structured script arduous and best left to collaborators. Whether or not one accepts this view, however, there seems little doubt that Altman has consistently reworked screenplays with intelligence, audacity and insight. Major works, such as *M*A*S*H*, *Nashville* and *The Player*, would be diminished without his script contributions.

Altman's decision to push *Death, Where is Thy Sting?* as a film appeared to be paying off when Cary Grant, who knew and admired Altman's work for television, became interested in the project. After a successful meeting with Grant, Altman, Wagner and Litto approached Mirisch, an independent production company (best known for its action hits *The Magnificent Seven* (1960) and *The Great Escape* (1963)) in partnership with United Artists, for financing. Altman filmed an aerial dogfight sequence as a showreel for potential investors, but neither Mirisch nor United Artists would accept him as a suitable director for a big budget Cary Grant vehicle (another problem may have been the unusual, highly episodic script. compared by Altman to the style of *M*A*S*H*).

The project fell into deeper trouble when Grant decided to pull out. Grant's career, it should be said, had been going through some odd phases. After a brief 'retirement' in the mid-fifties, the veteran star had resumed acting (most impressively in Hitchcock's *North by Northwest* (1959)) with as much success as before. In the early sixties, Grant became obsessed with appearing in a horror film (he approached producer/director Jack Clayton for a part in *The Innocents* (1961), based on Henry James' *The Turn of the Screw*, and Hammer Studios for the lead in *The Phantom of the Opera* (1962)). During the negotiations for *Death, Where is Thy Sting?*, he began to have doubts about acting at all, and, after a couple more appearances (*Father Goose* (1964); *Walk, Don't Run* (1966)) Grant retired from films for good.

Any lingering hopes Altman may have had about holding on to the project faded when Roald Dahl departed (Dahl's wife, actress Patricia Neal, was seriously ill at the time). Mirisch retained the rights to *Death, Where is Thy Sting?*, paying off its creators (Altman received $75,000). In 1965, the film went into production on location in Spain, with Gregory Peck in the leading role and David Miller (a competent but routine craftsman) directing. After ten days of shooting, adverse winter weather forced a shutdown in production. Mirisch opted to pull the plug on the film and *Death, Where is Thy Sting?* remains unmade.

Altman, in the meantime, attempted to initiate more projects, both for the cinema (a film version of the off-Broadway satire *MacBird*) and for television (*Our Man in Havana*). Unsuccessful, he picked up any bits and pieces of work available, including more television episodes (*Gunsmoke, Mr Novak*) and a second unit job directing a car chase sequence for *The Happening* (1967), a trendy 'caper' movie starring Anthony Quinn and Faye Dunaway. In 1966, Litto landed Altman some potentially more lucrative employment, as the director of a television pilot, *Nightwatch*. It is unlikely that Altman had any great enthusiasm for this police drama, but the location filming (in Chicago once again) meant relative freedom from executive producers and many of the production team were old friends: Lou Lombardo, Danford B. Greene, Brian McKay and Ray Wagner.

Things went smoothly until the post-production stage, when Wagner decided that the pilot needed re-editing. Altman disagreed and the argument was settled by Wagner's departure from *Nightwatch*. In return, Altman granted Wagner sole ownership of *Petulia*. The *Nightwatch* pilot found favour with the television executives but the projected series never materialized. Former employer Lucille Ball demanded its intended broadcast slot for her new series, *Mission Impossible*, and *Nightwatch* was cancelled. *Petulia*, on the other hand, passed into the hands of director Richard Lester (best known for his films with The Beatles, *A Hard Day's Night* (1964) and *Help* (1965)) and reached the screen in 1968, with Julie Christie, George C. Scott and Richard Chamberlain in the leading roles. Caught up in the ill feeling between Altman and Wagner, Litto opted to resign as the former's agent.

With his career at one of its all-time low points, Altman seemed as far away as ever from launching himself as a feature film director. Over ten years had passed since *The Delinquents*, and both *Death, Where is Thy Sting?* and *Petulia* were now only bitter reminders of what might have been. Salvation came in the unexpected form of an offer from Warner to direct a film about an American astronaut racing to be the first man on the moon.

Countdown was produced by Warner's low budget ($1 million per film) division, headed by executive producer William Conrad (also an actor, most notably in the television series *Cannon* (1971–5)). The producer, James Lydon, knew Altman from his *Kraft Theater* days at Universal and persuaded Conrad to take a chance on the director. Regarded as a risky choice, Altman had to promise to follow the script (by Loring Mandel) to the letter before being hired. He was, however, permitted some say in the casting, which apart from James Caan and Robert Duvall (both established actors but by no means stars) included television colleague Michael Murphy as a trainee astronaut.

The storyline of *Countdown* is relatively straightforward. A team of NASA astronauts, led by Chiz (Duvall), is in training for a projected moonshot when the news arrives that the Soviet Union is planning a moon landing in only a few days time. Chiz is the obvious choice to make a rival flight but it is decided that his military status (the cosmonauts are all civilians) makes him a politically unwise candidate. Lee Stegler (Caan), Chiz's back-up man, is selected in his place and undergoes an intensive period of training before being successfully launched into space.

After a credits sequence emphasizing the vast space hardware involved in the moon project (NASA co-operated with the production), *Countdown* unreels as a low-key, realistic drama which carefully balances the technology with the human side of the mission. The screenplay revolves around a series of conflicts: politics versus science (a fully-trained astronaut cannot be used for fear of upsetting international relations), science versus humanity/domesticity (Lee's family must suffer because of his mission and his own fears of failure) and Lee versus Chiz (the team leader resents the promotion of a less experienced man at his expense).

Established as both co-workers and close friends during the opening scene of the film (a mock space-flight), the relationship between Lee and Chiz is one of *Countdown*'s strongest elements. Chiz regards the mission to be first on the moon as rightfully his and looks on Lee's acceptance of it as an act of betrayal. He initially refuses to act as back-up for Lee (a reversal of their original positions) and tells him that he will fail. Lee accepts this resentment, arguing in return that the mission must take precedence over any personal feelings. Initially more objective than Chiz, he promises to back out if his chances of success do not look good. As his training progresses, however, Lee becomes gradually more stubborn and obsessive, even telling Chiz that he would have always been the wrong man for the mission, as he doesn't have the intelligence to succeed (as Peter Nicholls notes in *Fantastic Cinema*, the theme of an obsessed person following their dream is a recurrent Altman trademark). Though the two men eventually reach an understanding, their friendship seems irretrievably marred.

The domestic asides are a little more perfunctory, despite solid performances from Joanna Moore and Barbara Baxley as Lee and Chiz's respective wives, and mainly of interest for Mandel and Altman's emphasis on the stresses placed on Stegler's family while he makes history. Portrayed as content with the domestic duties of wife and mother, Mickey Stegler (Moore) is nevertheless strong-willed and independently-minded, unafraid to angrily turn on Lee when she realizes he has downplayed the risks of the mission. Lee's status as a media celebrity (the project gets leaked to the press) puts further pressure on Mickey, who feels she has been found wanting as the model wife of a hero-to-be (her parents are divorced). It is left to their son, Stevie, to remind Lee that his success will undermine his role as a husband and father (once on the moon, he must remain there until the next mission twelve months later). Lee's response to Mickey's anxieties is that his whole life now seems merely a build-up to the moon-flight; if he fails he becomes a nobody. His only gesture towards his family is to take his son's toy mouse with him on the flight.

The actual trip to the moon and subsequent landing appear to have engaged Altman's interest more than some of the earlier sequences. As the rocket door closes on Lee, the camera zooms in on the astronaut, now imprisoned in his capsule. During the actual flight in space, we never see the craft from the outside (Altman did not want to use models, presumably feeling them to be unrealistic.) Altman concentrates instead on Lee, often in close-up, isolated and scared (despite reassuring messages from ground control), with occasional views from the porthole. There is no concern here with the mystique of space travel, only the realities of a man operating under great stress and fear. The tension is increased by a malfunction which causes the spacecraft to lose electrical power. Instructed by ground control to switch off his radio for a period (to conserve energy), Lee at first refuses, unwilling to lose contact with the earth. As he cuts off communication, the interior of the capsule in semi-darkness, a press conference explaining the procedure of the mission is contrasted with the fraught reality.

The moon landing marks the point where Lee finally goes beyond his duties (whether as an astronaut, a patriot or a national celebrity) and acts for himself and his own sense of destiny. Orbiting the moon, he has orders not to attempt a landing unless he sights the beacon of a shelter (launched in a capsule six days before the manned flight) where he will live for the next year. The beacon does not appear, but rather than abort the mission, Lee pretends he has located it (his deception emphasized by a close-up of his sweating face) and lands. Contact with ground control is now lost entirely.

At the conclusion of *Countdown*, Lee's family, friends and colleagues (along with the rest of the world) believe that he has succeeded in being the first man on the moon at the cost of his own life. With only a few minutes of oxygen left, he'd failed to reach the shelter. Lee, however, is alive. Having spun the toy mouse on its elastic to determine his direction of travel, he sights the beacon (its red light reflected first on his watch, then on his helmet visor) just in time. His survival is contrasted with the fate of the Soviet cosmonauts, who in fact beat him to the moon, but died on leaving their spacecraft (presumably their spacesuits could not withstand the moon's lack of atmosphere). Lee lays out the American and Soviet flags together on a rock (if the moon belongs to anyone it must belong to everyone), along with the toy mouse, his only link to his family back on earth. The final image of the film, as the camera pulls back to a high-angled long shot, is of Lee striding towards the shelter and safety.

There is little in *Countdown* to suggest the style and themes of Altman's later films (though the examination of celebrity, touched on here, would figure prominently in *Nashville*). Most of the direction is unobtrusive and straightforward, with a few flashes of experimentation, such as the use of unstable, hand-held cameras for the press conference scene. There is some

Countdown – Lee (James Caan) takes a giant step

use of overlapping dialogue, which Lydon permitted after initial reservations. Altman's most individual touch, and the only source of contention with Lydon, is the ending, which is rather more ambiguous than the original script (so much for promises). The moon sequence is scientifically inaccurate, with near earth-type gravity and a none too convincing moonscape (in reality the Mojave Desert tinted, with a superimposed space backdrop), but the irony survives the dated special effects.

Rumours of studio interference, involving extensive re-shooting and re-editing, have tended to marginalize *Countdown* as a Robert Altman film. It is certainly difficult to slot it into his entire body of work, being for the most part a mainstream studio assignment. Altman's attitude to the film is fairly dismissive. He claims to have been fired from the production by Jack Warner himself after completing principal photography. Despite his protests, he was refused any control over the editing. As with the Hitchcock incident, there is an alternative version of events. In an interview with McGilligan, James Lydon claims that Jack Warner saw *Countdown* only after post-production was completed, liked it (his sole quibble being the overlapping dialogue) and had nothing more to do with the film. Even if Warner had disliked Altman's work, firing him would be pointless as he was on a one-film contract. William Conrad did film a few close-ups of Robert Duvall to smooth out the editing, but this (a standard studio practice) hardly qualifies as a major re-shoot.

Whatever the case, *Countdown* was released in 1968 (a year after filming was completed), as the bottom half of a double bill with the infamous *The Green Berets* (1968), aptly described by one critic as 'the Vietnam gospel according to Saint John Wayne'. Reviews were positive but the film quickly disappeared from view. A re-release the following year proved equally brief, leaving Altman dispirited.

His first big studio assignment completed, Altman now turned his back on television entirely. The delay in *Countdown*'s release (such as it was) brought both frustration and financial difficulties, yet he would reject offers of work on *Bonanza* or *The High Chaparral* rather than admit defeat. Two film projects seemed like possibilities. *A Spoonful of Love*, a Spanish-set tale of romance and LSD, got little further than Brian McKay's script. *At Lake Lugano*, the story of an Auschwitz survivor, attracted both a potential star, Anouk Aimée, and backing from Columbia. While Barbara Turner's screenplay proved popular with Aimée, however, Altman did not and Columbia dropped him from any possible deal. Turner attempted to continue with the project, without any success.

Countdown was still sitting on the shelf when, in late 1967, George Litto agreed to resume his former role as Altman's agent. Litto arranged a deal with Donald Factor (son and heir of cosmetics tycoon Max Factor), to part-finance *That Cold Day in the Park*, based on a new book Altman had optioned for filming. The book, by Richard Miles, was set in Paris, but Altman wanted to relocate the action to London. To this end he hired the British author Gillian Freeman to write the script (a successful novelist, Freeman had one previous screenplay, *The Leather Boys* (1963), to her credit). With Elizabeth Taylor under consideration for the lead (a sexually repressed middle-aged spinster), Columbia's London office was approached for the rest of the financing. No interest was shown (according to Freeman, the head of production did not even bother to hear the whole of the story pitch) and a deal was eventually made with the Canadian-based Commonwealth United.

Budgeted at $1.2 million ($700,000 from Commonwealth, $500,000 from Donald Factor), *That Cold Day in the Park* went into production in Vancouver in 1968. Free from any studio or union constraints, Altman had a fairly ideal set-up. The project was his own and he had a say in the choice of crew, which included Robert Eggenweiler and Danford B. Greene. A new member of his 'team' was art director Leon Ericksen, who would design several of Altman's major films (most spectacularly the entire town used in *McCabe and Mrs Miller*). The only source of trepidation for Altman came from working with star Sandy Dennis, his first 'big name'. Though not a media figure in the Elizabeth Taylor style, Dennis was a highly respected stage and film actress (winner of an Academy Award for her role in *Who's Afraid of Virginia Woolf?* (1966). Any worries Altman may have had proved groundless, however, and Dennis' skill at portraying insecure, often neurotic characters found an ideal vehicle in the role of Frances Austen.

A claustrophobic, often uncomfortable study of sexual repression and obsession, *That Cold Day in the Park* depicts the relationship between Frances and an un-named teenage boy (Michael Burns) she takes into her home after seeing him, alone and apparently homeless, on a park bench. At first, Frances adopts a maternal attitude to the silent boy, cooking for him and buying him new clothes. After a few days, it becomes clear she looks on him as a lover rather than a son. Unhappy with this, the boy attempts to leave, only to find all the doors locked and the windows nailed shut. Frances is going to keep him with her, whether he likes it or not.

Dressed in dull, 'sensible' clothes (emphasized by the film's sombre, subdued colours), Frances seems the archetypal film spinster, her largely solitary existence broken only by dull social activities (lunches with older friends and evenings at the bowling green). Though only in her early thirties, she seems to have already given up on life and gone into premature retirement. Her flat, though spacious, is as drab as her dress sense, and Altman often frames Frances through household objects, as if she was just another part of the furniture.

Frances' act of giving the boy shelter from the rain and cold seems initially to stem from kindness and compassion (contrasted with the uncaring attitude of some lunch guests who accuse her of excessive sentimentality). During this opening scene, which makes effective use of overlapping dialogue as we catch bits and pieces of banal lunchtime conversation, Altman repeatedly cuts away from the dinner table to shots from a window over-looking the park as Frances watches the boy. Once the guests have departed, she goes out to talk with him. Though well-meaning, it seems both naive and reckless of her to invite a stranger into her home and tell him to take his clothes off, albeit for a bath. This first meeting anticipates the later turn of events by separating the characters with a wire fence topped with barbs; a sense of confinement is already pervasive. Similarly, when Frances locks the door of the boy's bedroom later that night, what appears to be a precaution for self-protection is in fact his first taste of captivity.

Frances' sexual designs on the boy, which she does not articulate until relatively late on in the film, are heavily hinted at when, having unwittingly consumed some hash cookies (offered to her by the boy), she begins to play flirtatious games with him. A later visit to a gynaecologist confirms that she has more than a little innocuous romance in mind (she tells the doctor she is to be married). Frances is offered a more conventional relationship by Dr Charles Stevenson (one of the lunch guests) but shows no interest. As Charles talks earnestly of romance, Altman cuts to Frances' gynaecological examination earlier on, undermining his notions of love with the clinical realities. In a sad monologue (filmed in one continuous take), dwelling on loneliness, her dead mother and old age, Frances talks of her disgust at the thought of even being touched by Charles, an 'old man' (there is a tentative hint here of childhood abuse).

Sexual peculiarities are not confined to Frances. The boy, who makes a couple of covert excursions from the flat before being trapped, has a decidedly unusual relationship with his sister, Nina (Suzanne Benton). First seen (by both her brother and the viewer) engaged in copulation with a boyfriend, Nina orders her intruding brother out of the room, but does not seem bothered that he continues to watch through a window. Nina later makes an uninvited appearance at the flat, strips off in front of the boy and takes a bath while he watches (the nudity in the film, both male and female, is quite explicit for the period). She does not need to pull her brother in on top of her for the audience to get the point (but does so any-way) and it was a little heavy-handed of Freeman and Altman to have her bluntly ask the boy if she arouses him. It is not clear how this unconsum-mated incest is supposed to relate to Frances' desire for the boy (he is merely exchanging one perverse relationship for another), and ultimately it seems included mainly for extra weirdness and titillation.

In the final section of *That Cold Day in the Park*, where the boy reveals to Frances that he can talk after all (his silence is a somewhat contrived device, explained away as merely a childhood habit he has retained), the already peculiar atmosphere gets steadily more bizarre. Frances, having decided that the boy will agree to stay with her if he is regularly provided with sexual partners other than herself, procures the services of a prostitute (Luana Anders) and locks her in with him (Altman is careful to deglamorize the prostitute, introducing her in a seedy bar and framing her through a bathroom doorway as she sits on a lavatory to undress for work). Midway through their rather unenthusiastic coupling, Frances attacks the woman, stabbing her to death with a kitchen knife. The films ends with an extreme close-up of the boy's terrified face as Frances soothes him with promises of security and love.

As Altman's first truly personal work, *That Cold Day in the Park* is as intriguing as it is flawed. His style is at its most 'fly-on-the-wall' here, most noticeably in the scene at the gynaecologist's, where the camera looks in through the waiting room window at Frances, while a couple of women to her right discuss various forms of contraception. Altman's use of the slow zoom, combined with the framing effect of windows and doorways, reinforces the impression that we are distanced observers looking at real events the camera has merely chanced upon. When the boy pays a brief visit to his family, the camera remains outside, but cranes up the front of the house to peek at the life within. The camerawork (by Laszlo Kovacs) can be a little

That Cold Day in the Park – Frances (Sandy Dennis)

restless and Altman does on occasion mistake out-of-focus shots of kitchen-ware for atmosphere or style, but in general the direction is assured. Another strength is Johnny Mandel's score, which incorporates a strange, musical-box-style motif suggesting childhood memories and nostalgia for a better, safer time.

Critical response to *That Cold Day in the Park* was mixed, ranging from enthusiastic (if puzzled) to John Simon's terse dismissal: 'about as preten-tious, loathsome and stupid as a film can get'. Several reviewers disliked the climactic violence (although it is anticipated by a scene where the boy dis-covers a doll which Frances has torn apart in a rage), regarding it as more appropriate to a schlock horror movie in the *Whatever Happened to Baby Jane?* (1962) tradition than a supposedly serious study of a disturbed mind. Little seen on its original, minimal release, *That Cold Day in the Park* is probably of most interest now as a forerunner of Altman's two other 'strange women with violent tendencies' films, *Images* and *Three Women*. As with the main characters in these dramas, the figure of Frances Austen, though fascinating, remains ultimately beyond our comprehension.

Images, a subjective account of a woman undergoing violent mental disin-tegration, was in fact intended as an immediate follow-up to *That Cold Day in the Park*, to be filmed in Vancouver with finance from a Texas million-aire. James Lydon agreed to act as producer, though he had doubts about Altman's script (one of the director's very few solo efforts). The backer withdrew before production could get underway, leaving Altman wonder-ing if his film career was about to grind to another halt. By 1969, he was seriously considering an offer of another television series pilot (from, surprisingly, his old Universal nemesis, Roy Huggins) when a film script he had admired but never expected to be offered came his way.

*M*A*S*H*, Altman's best-known film and his one big box-office success, remains his most important film from a career point of view. Without it, he could never have gained the opportunity to embark on the incredibly pro-lific and creative period of work which followed. Subsequent films were sometimes superior, but few were profitable and Altman's talent would have counted for little in Hollywood without the receipts from *M*A*S*H*.

If anyone had anticipated the film's success, Altman would not have even been considered as its director. The screenplay, by Ring Lardner Jr. (taken from a newly published novel by 'Richard Hooker', a pseudonym for H. Richard Hornberger), had been bought by Ingo Preminger (brother of director/producer Otto Preminger), an agent turned producer based at Twentieth Century Fox. Both Lardner and Preminger regarded *M*A*S*H* as a hot property but a succession of directors (including George Roy Hill, Stanley Kubrick, Sidney Lumet and over ten others) rejected it, mainly on the grounds that it was essentially a series of self-contained episodes (or vignettes) rather than a conventional linear narrative. George Litto, who happened to be Lardner's agent, suggested Altman to Preminger and screened *That Cold Day in the Park* for him. Impressed by both the director and the film, Preminger persuaded the less enthusiastic Fox executives, Richard Zanuck and David Brown, to hire Altman.

Preoccuped with the production of two epic-scale war films, *Patton* (1969) and *Tora, Tora, Tora* (1970), both budgeted at around $20 million, and a $24 million musical, *Hello Dolly* (1969), Zanuck and Brown contracted Altman for a minimal fee ($75,000), with no share in any profits, and left him to get on with the filming under Preminger's supervision. Costing only $3.5 million, with no stars (though Elliott Gould, Academy Award nominated for his role in *Bob and Carol and Ted and Alice* (1969), was an up-and-coming leading man), *M*A*S*H* was shot on location at Fox's Lake Malibu ranch, twenty miles from the studio headquarters (and any prying executives). The leading actors (Sutherland, Gould, Tom Skerritt and Sally Kellerman) were all cast by Preminger. Altman selected most of the background cast (using actors from an improvised-theatre company in San Francisco) and employed several of his 'regular' crew, including Danford B. Greene (his last collaboration with the director before being replaced by Lou Lombardo) and Leon Ericksen. The only major traumas during the ten weeks of filming involved the dismissal of the studio-appointed director of photography (who would not go along with Altman's desired visual style) and complaints from Sutherland and Gould, both of whom felt that Altman was giving them inadequate direction. Altman managed to make peace with Gould (who would star in two more films for Altman), but Sutherland remained unhappy and did not work with the director again.

Set during the Korean War (1950–3), *M*A*S*H* follows the experiences of Captain 'Hawkeye' Pierce (Sutherland), a surgeon stationed at the 4077th Mobile Army Surgical Hospital, along with his friends and colleagues 'Trapper' John McIntyre (Gould) and Duke Forrest (Skerritt). While dedicated as doctors, the men do not care for the idiocies of their military regime (an attitude former Army Air Force lieutenant Altman could appreciate) and seek release in various anarchic escapades which make up the main episodes of the film. A humourless religious hypocrite, Major Frank Burns (Robert Duvall), is taunted over his furtive extramarital affair until he goes beserk, while his mistress, Margaret 'Hotlips' Houlihan (Kellerman), an uptight military careerist, is publicly humiliated several times over. The resident dentist, 'Painless' Waldowski (John Schuck), suicidal over his fear of being impotent (and therefore no longer a real man), is cured by an arranged night of therapeutic sexual bliss with the appropriately named Lieutenant Dish (Jo Ann Pflug). After a brief trip to Japan, where Hawkeye and Trapper John indulge in a little golf and some major surgery on a congressman's GI son, things are rounded off with an all-American football game which the M*A*S*H team win through sheer determination and a lot of cheating.

Still a potent (if no longer shocking) black comedy, M*A*S*H's main achievement, as Danny Peary notes (in his *Guide for the Film Fanatic*), is to convince the viewer that characters who indulge in childish antics are also responsible professionals dealing with terrible casualties under great stress. Only a short distance from the hospital, men are daily shredded by bullets and shrapnel, damage which Hawkeye and his friends must repair. The film opens with an aerial shot of army helicopters, not here machines of war but a vital means of transporting wounded soldiers to the M*A*S*H base. The scenes in the operating theatre are gruesomely realistic, including one still unsettling moment when Hawkeye calmly sets about repairing a severed neck artery while blood jets into the air (far more effective than the heavy-handed gore, eviscerations and all, of the year's other military black comedy, *Catch 22*).

As well as being anti-military (though it never explicitly condemns either the Korean War or the then ongoing Vietnam conflict), M*A*S*H is also decidedly anti-religious (this bias, present in more marginal form in *McCabe and Mrs Miller* and *A Wedding*, has inevitably been interpreted as Altman's reaction against his Catholic education). Aside from Frank Burns (whose Bible-reading Korean pupil is easily distracted by Duke's copy of *Playboy*), there is the resident priest, Father 'Dago Red' Mulcahy (Rene Auberjonois). Primarily a source of comedy relief, Mulcahy's assistance with operations is shown to be of far more value than his religious duties (Hawkeye disrupts his ministrations over a dead soldier to get his help with one still living). Similarly, it is Hawkeye, not Mulcahy, who turns Waldowski's thoughts away from suicide (the mock farewell party held for the dentist is staged like a parody of the Last Supper, complete with bread and wine), even though the priest is the first to learn of the dentist's trauma.

The dialogue overlaps as never before (with conversation from one scene carried over well into the next). The visual style, incorporating the expected slow zooms and a slightly hazy look, is largely camouflage greens and browns, broken up by splashes of bright colour (Hawaiian shirts, golfing trousers, kimonos and spurting blood). Altman tries a few new techniques, such as a flash forward to an airport welcome when Duke hears he's being sent home. His main innovation here is the use of onscreen loudspeaker announcements as a means of linking (and punctuating) the film's various episodes (similar devices are employed in *Brewster McCloud*

M*A*S*H – Trapper John (Elliott Gould) and Hawkeye (Donald Sutherland)

and *Nashville*). The last of these announcements informs us that the film we have just seen is *M*A*S*H*, with a story full of 'zany antics', and lists the cast. In many films, this would be irritatingly self-referential, but here it reinforces the circular nature of the script, which begins and ends with Hawkeye and Duke driving off in a (stolen) jeep. Also crucial to the film's success is Johnny Mandel's theme music, its melancholy style complemented by some odd lyrics (written by Altman's son Michael), including the famous line 'Suicide is painless, It brings on many changes'.

M*A*S*H's only serious flaw, the overlong football sequence aside, lies with a number of characters the film seems unsure what to do with. Duke Forrest, a 'good ole boy' from the Deep South, is set up as a major character at the same time as Hawkeye. Once Trapper John has appeared, however, Duke tends to fade into the background, eventually becoming fairly irrelevant to the proceedings. He is never particularly likeable (being sexist, racist and grinning like an idiot) and it is no real loss when he gives up centre stage to Trapper John.

More problematic is the character of Hotlips. Described by Trapper John as 'the sultry bitch with the fire in her eyes', she is depicted as an establishment figure to be mocked. Her night of passion with Frank Burns is relayed over the entire base via a strategically-placed microphone. While she takes a shower, the screen is pulled away so that Hawkeye and friends (most of the M*A*S*H personnel) can determine whether or not she is a natural blonde. Hawkeye's eventual admission of respect for Hotlips, 'You may be a pain in the ass, but you're a damn good nurse', seems little more than a token gesture, especially as it comes before the 'shower humiliation' scene. According to McGilligan, Lardner's script had Hotlips depart after the shower incident. Altman retains the character, making her 'one of the gang', without explaining her abrupt change in attitude (she even has a very unconvincing fling with Duke). During the football sequence, acting as one of the cheerleaders, Hotlips' ignorance of the game's rules makes her the continued butt of people's jokes. Altman has defended M*A*S*H against criticisms of misogyny, claiming that he was merely reflecting the attitudes to women prevalent at the time. This is at odds with another claim that he did not intend to give the film a specific time and place (only mentioning Korea at Fox's insistence). Furthermore, this misogyny is displayed by characters (Hawkeye, Trapper John) we are supposed to admire for their sensitivity.

Both Altman and Preminger were convinced that M*A*S*H would be a hit. Zanuck and Brown, on the other hand, disliked the film and ordered a complete re-edit. Preminger persuaded them to first preview Altman's cut of M*A*S*H in San Francisco. The audience proved ecstatic and the film was released in its original version. Post-*Easy Rider*, Dennis Hopper's 1969 drugs and bikes and rock 'n' roll movie, anti-establishment films were briefly popular with moviegoers and M*A*S*H must have seemed anarchic in both form and content. M*A*S*H eventually grossed around $40 million for Fox. It also won several major awards, including the *Palme d'or* at Cannes and an Academy Award for Best Screenplay (plus nominations for Best Picture, Best Director, Best Supporting Actress and Best Editing). Altman's career was up and running. He took no share of M*A*S*H's profits (nor did he make anything from the subsequent television series) and would later claim to have contributed rather more to the script than the loudspeaker links (Ring Lardner's Academy Award win may have exacerbated any feelings of resentment over writing credits) but for now Altman could enjoy his success; the doors of the big Hollywood studios were finally open.

4

Beautiful Dreamers: McCloud, McCabe & Cathryn

Following *M*A*S*H*, Altman might have been expected to embark on one of his own projects rather than rely on George Litto to find him an existing production looking for a director. Instead, he agreed to take on a script which had been drifting from studio to studio since 1967. *Brewster McCloud's Sexy Flying Machine*, written by Doran William Cannon, had been purchased by first-time producer Lou Adler as a potentially lucrative 'youth' picture, which took as its theme the quest for freedom in an oppressive society (Adler subsequently co-produced the slightly less portentous *Rocky Horror Picture Show* (1975)). Metro Goldwyn Mayer, though in a precarious financial position, was providing the backing. Working through his own company, Lion's Gate (named after a bridge just outside Vancouver), for the first time, Altman requested and received complete artistic control (despite the fact that *M*A*S*H* had not yet been released to prove his bankability). He relocated the film to Houston (Cannon's screenplay was set in New York) and then proceeded to rewrite large sections of the script (Brian McKay did some work on the film, but quit after deciding that he did not know what Altman wanted). Oddly enough, the production suffered the same difficulties as *M*A*S*H*: a change in cameraman (Lamar Boren replacing Jordan Cronenweth) and a discontented leading man.

With *Brewster McCloud* (1970), Altman seems to have been trying to outdo the quirkiness, anarchy, black humour and satire (among other things) of *M*A*S*H*. It promotes several of that film's supporting cast – Sally Kellerman, Rene Auberjonois, Bud Cort and Michael Murphy – to starring roles. Sadly, for all its inventiveness and amusing moments, *Brewster McCloud* falls flat. Much of the would-be offbeat humour is laboured or just plain unfunny. Too many of its ideas and styles seem like leftovers from *M*A*S*H* re-served in an unappetizing mix. Visually rather dull, the film is also let down by Altman's direction, which despite his great expertise is on occasion both careless and lazy.

The plot concerns Brewster McCloud (Cort), an odd young man who lives (secretly) in the Houston Astrodome, devoting all his time to the planning and construction of a pair of mechanical wings. Brewster is convinced that his only means of escape from the corrupt, bigoted world he lives in is to literally fly away. He is guided in his quest by Louise (Kellerman), an even more peculiar woman who watches over him, protecting him from anyone who threatens his work. Meanwhile, Houston police are baffled by a series of killings where each victim is found strangled and covered in bird droppings. A celebrated San Francisco detective, Frank Shaft (Murphy) is called in by an ambitious local politician to advise on the case. The trail eventually leads to Brewster, who takes off with his wings just as the police corner him in the Astrodome.

The various goings-on in *Brewster McCloud* are linked by a series of lectures on birds and bird behaviour delivered in an unspecified setting to an unseen audience. The lecturer (Auberjonois), whose first words ('I forgot the opening line') replace the MGM Lion's traditional roar, establishes the film's theme – man's dream of flight and the freedom offered by flight – and continues to comment (either in person or as a voiceover) on the unfolding plot and characters. An entertaining figure, the lecturer becomes more birdlike himself as the film progresses, finally evolving into a bird/human hybrid. He never interacts with the other characters, though, and his segments (greatly expanded by Altman from the screenplay) seem mainly a means of joining the bits and pieces of main plot(s) which would otherwise fall apart into a paceless mess.

The lecturer explains Brewster's mission. Louise shows him the methods he must follow in order to succeed. Dressed only in a raincoat and sporting scars on her back where wings might once have sprouted (she is, after all, Brewster's guardian angel), she warns Brewster to keep away from girls. Sex is merely a poor substitute for flying. Worse, it ties people to the earth, depriving them of their childhood yearning (and capacity) for flight. Appearing on the fringes of many scenes, Louise is obviously connected to the offscreen murders (most of the victims, aside from being racist, sexist, fascist, homophobic and anti-Semitic, represent a direct threat to Brewster). Despite her devotion to Brewster, she abandons him when he breaks her command not to indulge in sex, as he has both betrayed her trust and thrown away his chance of true freedom.

The temptations of sex are represented by the two other women in Brewster's life. Hope (Jennifer Salt), who works in a health food store and supplies Brewster with nutrition, is aroused by the sight of him working out (for his flight) and masturbates underneath the Stars and Stripes (an illegal act in some American States) as he trains. Suzanne (Shelley Duvall in her acting debut), a tour guide at the Astrodome, initiates Brewster into the joys of sex. Brewster wants Suzanne to fly away with him (for all Louise's warnings, he seems not to realize that he's now bound to the earth) but when he tells her about his wings, she appreciates them only in terms of money and patent rights. It is a tribute to Duvall's talent that the gangly, wide-eyed Suzanne, essentially just a collection of arbitrary eccentricities (such as her abilities as an amateur racing driver), comes across as an interesting character. Some of her dialogue, droning on about food and dinner parties, anticipates her role in *Three Women*. Other parts of the script, as when she is required to throw up and then passionately kiss a boyfriend on the lips, are decidedly ill-advised.

In comparison to his supporting characters, Brewster McCloud himself is regrettably dull, a dead centre from which the film never recovers. A number of key Altman protagonists (John McCabe, Philip Marlowe, Essex (in *Quintet*), Popeye, Vincent Van Gogh) are obsessive, idiosyncratic but honourable outsiders (also, one suspects, Altman's image of himself), yet Brewster never even begins to come alive on the screen. Bud Cort retains the same blank expression throughout, and it is difficult to care whether or not he succeeds in attaining his goal. It does not help that this goal seems pointless to say the least. Flight may equate with freedom but all birds must return to earth eventually. A shot of a dead dove lying in a graveyard serves as an omen of Brewster's own unfortunate ending.

In the not-so-grand finale, Brewster flaps about the enclosed Astrodome, while on the soundtrack the lecturer informs us that man can never attain mastery of the air, as it takes millions of years of evolution. Lacking the 'self-contained mechanism', true flight will always be beyond his capabilities. To illustrate this point, Brewster (whose wings, designed by Leon Ericksen, are impressive but impractical) quickly tires out and, screaming, falls to his death, a pathetic modern Icarus. His dream was always an empty, futile one. As if to underline the arbitrariness of the whole enterprise, Altman concludes with a bizarre parade (described by McGilligan as 'Fellini-esque'), bringing on the rest of the cast (dressed as circus acts) to assemble around Brewster's corpse. The actors having been announced *à la M*A*S*H*, we finish with a medium close-up of the smashed body, half-concealed by the wrecked wings. This still stands as the most tasteless moment in any Altman film.

The overabundance of bird imagery (it is difficult to respect a film whose chief visual motif is bird shit) and crass cinematic in-jokes (incorporating both old movie references and the process of film-making itself) do not help the proceedings. When the title song (the American anthem) is messed up, the camera resumes its initial position and the credits restart with the music. Aside from a number of *Wizard of Oz* (1939) references,

Brewster McCloud

such as casting Margaret Hamilton (the Wicked Witch of the West) as one of the victims and dressing Hope in Judy Garland/Dorothy-style costumes, the major in-joke is the character of Shaft. A parody of the Steve McQueen character in *Bullitt* (1968), complete with noisy car, piercing blue eyes (which turn out to be contact lenses), numerous turtleneck sweaters and a choice of leather shoulder holsters, Shaft was added to the script by Altman to provide Michael Murphy with a role. This accounts for his irrelevance to the proceedings, a fact underlined by his unexpected suicide well before the end of the film (he shoots himself after crashing his car into a pond).

Variously described as a Victorian fable in the style of a *Roadrunner* cartoon (the *New Yorker*), a twisted fairytale (Peary) and a weird hippy shit film (Kim Newman in *Nightmare Movies*), *Brewster McCloud* failed at the box office. To be fair, it was already doomed before its release. Metro Goldwyn Mayer underwent a change in management and the new studio head, the late James Aubrey, disliked the film intensely. After token distribution, *Brewster McCloud* was withdrawn from circulation. It has since acquired a certain cult reputation, though, in Altman's own words, all a cult really means is not enough people to make a minority.

The disappointment of *Brewster McCloud* did little to impede Altman's career (released in the same year as *M°A°S°H*, it was completely over-shadowed by the runaway success of the latter film). Mirisch approached the director, offering him the chance to resurrect *Death, Where is Thy Sting?*. Having fallen out with the project's writer, Brian McKay, over the *Brewster McCloud* screenplay, Altman now had little enthusiasm for the idea. After a few pre-production discussions he backed out.

During the shooting of *Brewster McCloud*, McKay had been working on the screenplay for *McCabe and Mrs Miller*, Altman's next production (based on a 1959 novel, *McCabe*, by Edmund Naughton, considered by several studios for film adaptation). A decidedly offbeat western, the film came to Altman via David Foster, a producer at Warner. Warren Beatty and Julie Christie took the leading roles, Altman's first real 'stars' since Sandy Dennis in *That Cold Day in the Park* (Altman originally wanted Elliott Gould for McCabe, but finance could not be secured without Beatty's participation). Beatty's most recent film, *The Only Game in Town* (1970), had proved a flop, and he was in need of a hit to maintain the status he had acquired as the producer/star of *Bonnie and Clyde* (1967).

The production of *McCabe and Mrs Miller* was both difficult and (by Altman's standards) protracted. The filming, on location in Vancouver, lasted from October 1970 to January 1971. The freezing winter weather (with frequent rain and snowstorms), aside from being tough on the cast and crew, brought technical difficulties such as highly variable sound quality. Altman rewrote sections of McKay's script, as did local writer Joseph Calvelli, a retired Hollywood scenarist responsible for another downbeat western, *Death of a Gunfighter* (1969). Robert Towne, who later wrote the screenplays for *Chinatown* (1974) and *Shampoo* (1975), contributed several ideas, while Beatty and Christie devised many of their own lines. Beatty, used to having numerous retakes to develop his performance, found it hard to adjust to Altman's film-making style and did not always get on with his director. Yet for all these difficulties, *McCabe and Mrs Miller* emerged as Altman's finest film so far.

The basic story element of *McCabe and Mrs Miller* would be at home in many a Hollywood western produced in the previous thirty years. A mysterious stranger, John Q. McCabe, rides into a small mining town, looking to make some money. A professional gambler (and reputed gunfighter), he sets up a small brothel. A high-class madam, Constance Miller, offers him a partnership and their business flourishes. A large mining company decides to move in on them. McCabe rejects their insultingly low offer and the company sends in three hired gunfighters to take care of him. Mrs Miller pleads with McCabe to leave town and start again elsewhere. McCabe refuses, electing instead to face the killers for a showdown.

Having assembled a number of familiar western ingredients (though pre-1960, prostitutes would be referred to as 'showgirls' or 'saloon entertainers'), Altman imbues them with a remarkable freshness and sense of authenticity. He explained his approach as simply taking a different perspective on the classic ingredients (or clichés) of the genre, the story being 'an easy clothes-line for me to hang my own essays on'. Forsaking the rugged, near-desert terrain of many a western epic, he locates the mining town, Presbyterian Church, among vast hills and forests, whose verdant greens and browns alternate with the blue-white chill of the frequent snowfall. Still under construction (and therefore new territory for business exploitation), the town is depicted in largely golden-brown imagery, sunlight and lamplight reflecting off the new timbers. The exquisite photography (by Vilmos Zsigmond, Altman's original choice for $M^\circ A^\circ S^\circ H$) is in marked contrast to the fairly dismal lives depicted. On the soundtrack, songs by Leonard Cohen (taken from an album not written specially for the film) provide a melancholy accompaniment.

The townspeople (among them Rene Auberjonois, John Schuck and Shelley Duvall) are all recently-arrived immigrants dressed in European clothes and retaining their national accents (Altman's own ancestors, the German-Dutch Altmanns, emigrated to the United States in the mid-nineteenth century). Most work at the nearby zinc mine and Presbyterian Church is little more than a place to sleep at night. This lack of any real sense of community is underlined by the absence of family groups (though one miner takes a mail-order wife and a young black couple arrive later on) and, as Geoff Andrew notes, no sign of a sheriff. For an extra touch of authenticity, Altman instructed the supporting cast to choose their own costumes from the period wardrobe provided (this enabled him to determine the personality of each actor) and make any necessary repairs themselves. The wide Panavision frame permits this wealth of background detail and activity without too much cutting away (and thereby digressing) from the main image and narrative.

Into this world rides John McCabe (his first sight of the town is, appropriately, the church itself). Sporting a bowler hat and big cigar in place of a cowboy's stetson and cheroot, McCabe heads straight for the saloon, run by Patrick Sheehan (Auberjonois), to set up a poker game. Hidden underneath the hat and a beard, Beatty's confident, slightly smug star persona shines through at this point. Here McCabe is in control, quickly attracting the interest of the assembled miners. As the film progresses he finds himself increasingly out of his depth. It is also here that the rumour of McCabe's gunfighter past starts. Sheehan, noticing the gambler's gun, whispers that this is the man who shot Bill Roundtree.

Having announced himself as a businessman, McCabe purchases three downmarket whores ($80 a piece) and launches his brothel with the women working from makeshift tents. This modest enterprise runs into trouble when one whore goes berserk and stabs a client. It takes English madam Constance Miller (Mr Miller's whereabouts are not explained) to turn McCabe's dream of business success into reality. Dealing in 'class girls and clean linen' (and available herself for the top price of $5), she offers McCabe an equal partnership. Their brothel soon has a reputation as the best in the territory.

For all his amorality, McCabe is a curiously touching figure, his cockiness masking a naivety about the harsh realities of big business which proves his undoing. Having rejected the offer made by two agents of the Harris and Shaughnessey Mining Company, he confidently waits for an improved bid. Mrs Miller knows full well that he is just as likely to get shot in the back. Even when convinced of his dangerous position, he seeks advice from a lawyer (William Devane), who thinks only in meaningless abstracts and ideals, rather than a means of escape. Altman regards McCabe as an attractive character because he is aware of his own failings and limitations. Though in love with Mrs Miller, and conscious of the 'poetry' this inspires within him, McCabe knows he hasn't the ability to put his feelings into words.

Mrs Miller is an altogether less sympathetic figure (it doesn't help that Julie Christie's otherwise assured performance is impaired by occasional lapses into Hollywood Cockney). Hard-headed in business (far more so than McCabe), she confronts the realities of frontier life without flinching. When Ida Coyl (Shelley Duvall) is widowed, she takes her on as a whore, telling her that it's just the same as being a mail-order wife. In both instances, sex pays for her bed and board. Even McCabe must pay the $5 for Mrs Miller's services. As they get down to business, Altman zooms in on the cashbox by her bedside (which, as Kolker notes, is the only 'heart of gold' this whore possesses). When she finally allows McCabe into her bed without charge, it is to comfort him rather than reciprocate his love. She cares about him getting hurt but cannot understand his determination to resist the might of the mining company.

With the arrival of the hired killers (first seen on horseback, silhouetted against a backlit forest), led by Dog Butler (Hugh Millais), *McCabe and Mrs Miller* takes on a more brutal tone (the death of Ida's husband is largely obscured by shadow). In a highly unnerving scene, McCabe tries to explain to the giant-sized Butler that he is now willing to negotiate with the company. Butler refuses to talk business with him, explaining that he is only in town for some hunting (true enough). Butler tests McCabe by pretending to be a friend (of a friend) of the late Bill Roundtree, concluding that he will be an easy victim ('That man never killed anybody').

We are given a taste of the violence McCabe must face when one of Butler's henchmen, a young 'punk' (Manfred Schulz) who in appearance and attitude resembles a scruffy Nazi youth, murders an amiable cowboy (Keith Carradine) as he crosses a rope bridge. This senseless act of aggression is followed by a slow motion death plunge, which we witness from above, as the cowboy falls into an icy river. This is a man who meant nothing to the company. We can only dread to think what will happen to someone they regard as an enemy.

McCabe and Mrs Miller

As Mrs Miller sinks into oblivion in an opium den (she keeps her drug abuse a secret, a curious attitude for someone who makes a living from other people's vices), the showdown between McCabe and the killers commences. A snowstorm is in progress, giving the scene the look of a Bruegel winter landscape, McCabe seeks to defend himself from the vantage point of the church, but is thrown out by the pastor (up until now a barely-glimpsed character). This anti-religious slant is enforced when, later on, the townspeople rush to save the burning church, ignoring McCabe's dying struggle. The pastor's callous act rebounds on him as Butler shoots him in mistake for McCabe (Altman employs an effective burst of extreme violence here, showing the pastor's right arm dangling from his body by a few shreds of flesh). As McCabe is stalked through the snow (a lot of this sequence was shot by editor Lou Lombardo and assistant director Tommy Thompson), he manages to ambush all three of the killers (not hesitating to shoot one in the back). Hit by three bullets, his own death and burial by the snow can be read, as Peary suggests, as a purification of McCabe, a vindication of his decision to fight. He is also being obliterated from the mind of Mrs Miller. Altman cuts from McCabe's corpse to a close up of her eye focused on an opium bottle in her hand. This bottle (the film's final image) now encompasses her entire world. McCabe, from Altman's point of view, has gambled and both won (his integrity) and lost (the woman he loves and his own life).

Shot under difficult conditions, *McCabe and Mrs Miller* then went on to face damning previews. A rushed release schedule had led to the prints being incorrectly processed, with poor colour and unintelligible sound. Some positive reviews (including one from influential critic Pauline Kael) followed once the corrected prints were released, but too late to help the film's commercial chances. Despite this failure, producer David Foster retained his enthusiasm for esoteric westerns, acquiring a script by newcomer Michael Cimino entitled *The Johnson County War*. Eight years later, the project finally went into production under a new title, *Heaven's Gate*.

Altman now made a brief departure from Hollywood in order to finally film his *Images* script. No American studio had shown any interest in financing the project and so it was expedience rather than choice which led Altman to work abroad for the first time. A British company, Hemdale, put up the modest budget (under $1 million), and filming took place in Ireland at the Ardmore studios, with location shooting at a country house in County Wicklow. Susannah York agreed to play the difficult leading role (though she felt the original script to be overly enigmatic) with *McCabe and Mrs Miller* actors Rene Auberjonois and Hugh Millais in supporting roles.

The minimal plot (reworked by Altman and his cast throughout the filming) centres around Cathryn (York), a beautiful but disturbed woman suffering from an ever-advancing mental disorder which manifests itself as a series of vivid hallucinations. A voice on the telephone tells her of an affair her husband, Hugh (Auberjonois), is having. When Hugh appears she mistakes him for a former lover, Rene (Marcel Bozzuffi), now dead. During a weekend break at her childhood home in the countryside, the hallucinations intensify. Rene continues to appear, while Hugh and a visiting friend, Marcel (Millais) become interchangeable. On top of all this, Cathryn also begins to hallucinate a doppelganger, who pursues her from a distance. After apparently 'killing' this double, she believes she had freed herself from her inner demons.

Images is a bold, disturbing film which, depending on the viewer's mood, can seem either a perceptive look at the nature of madness and its root causes or a pretentious, overly-arty charade amounting to very little (the element of game-playing is accentuated by having each actor take another cast member's name for their character). Altman has cited both Ingmar Bergman's *Persona* (1966), with its identity switches, and Joseph Losey's 'psycho-drama' *Secret Ceremony* (1968) as his inspiration, yet the resulting work is neither homage nor imitation. At times the film seems to be operating in an unfathomable no-man's-land between the case-study approach of Roman Polanski's *Repulsion* (1965) and the outright dreamscape of *Three Women*.

Images' most daring stroke is to employ a subjective point of view for nearly all of its running time. Having established Cathryn as a children's author specializing in fantasy (the text used is from *In Search of Unicorns*, a book written by York), the film then makes us share her perception of the world. Thus her hallucinations, or images, are as real to the viewer as the rest of the film. This enforced intimacy allows for some jolting effects (when Hugh first turns into Rene, we jump as much as Cathryn) and a sustained sense of disorientation. The downside of this approach is that events tend to get a little confusing (though the 'reality', or otherwise, of what we see is usually clarified) with even the film's setting left unclear. Altman uses readings from *In Search of Unicorns* and a jigsaw puzzle depicting a country house (gradually completed over the course of the film) in a fashion that recalls the loudspeakers of *M°A°S°H* and the lectures of *Brewster McCloud*, but the exact purpose of these devices remains defiantly obscure.

The voice on the phone (clearly her own, though nothing is made of this) reflects Cathryn's fears of losing her relationship with Hugh (possibly she equates a stable marriage with stability in her mind) and a lack of faith in his fidelity. Rene, after his startling first appearance, serves mostly as an ironic commentator on Cathryn's confused existence, laughing at the idea of being a ghost. This bizarre relationship even develops a little grim humour as Cathryn brains him with a heavy ornament and then complains that his bleeding will ruin the furnishings. Marcel, who exists both as a real character and an 'image', is a more disturbing figure. Another former lover of Cathryn, her hallucinations of him involve an explicit element of sado-masochism. This notion of Cathryn as a passive victim of men's selfish demands is reinforced in a scene where she makes love to Rene (either a flashback or a hallucination) who transforms first into Marcel, then Hugh and then himself again. Her response is to blast Rene with her husband's shotgun and stab Marcel in the neck with a kitchen knife (an action neatly telegraphed by the sound of the blade being sharpened). After both bloody events, the respective images disappear (the 'real' Marcel turns up the next day alive and well).

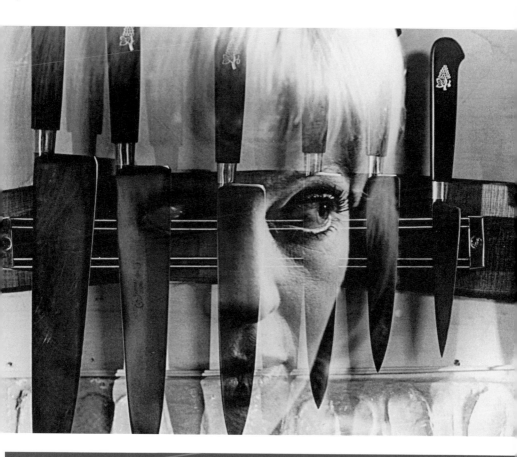

Images – Cathryn (Susannah York) with trouble in mind

The idea of mental wellbeing through cathartic (if imagined) violence loses some of its coherence with the introduction of the doppelganger. Unlike the other images, Cathryn has no interaction with this remote figure until the film's last few minutes when it finally draws near. Determined to free her mind, Cathryn rams the double with her car, sending it over a waterfall (a recurring motif). Any sense of release is shortlived when, having returned home, she is confronted by the figure once more. Altman then abandons the subjective point of view, taking us back to the waterfall, where Hugh's battered corpse lies in the rocks below. Though an effective shock moment, this finale undermines much of what has gone before. The images are as potent as ever, and have now led to a killing where the body cannot be imagined away.

Also problematic is Cathryn's relationship with Susannah (Cathryn Harrison), Marcel's daughter. Blonde and pale-skinned, she is clearly intended to represent a younger version of Cathryn, as yet untroubled by the burdens and pressures of womanhood. There is a suggestion that Susannah is fated to follow Cathryn down the road of insanity (at one point their faces merge as the girl's reflection is superimposed over Cathryn's face in a car window) but ultimately this seems merely a touch of self-indulgent despair.

For all its beautiful autumnal surroundings (photographed by Vilmos Zsigmond), Cathryn's childhood home, with its cold blue/grey interiors, offers little in the way of comfort. She seems to find peace only in her children's fantasy. We see her lying on a bed, curled up in a foetal position, with pages of her book scattered about her. Even after the very real murder of her husband, we return to the book. As the final part is heard on the soundtrack, the jigsaw is finished, revealing a unicorn standing outside the country house. The search is over.

Altman's style in *Images* can be as disorientating as his content, making much use of relentless zooms, fast pans and disjointed editing. York is often kept in tight close-up, the camera pursuing her as she paces about. John Williams' music is all ominous piano and strings, disrupted by discordant, oriental-style sounds courtesy of Stomu Yamash'ta.

If *Images* finally survives its multiple confusions and pretensions, it is because of Susannah York's performance, which runs a formidable gamut of vulnerability, tenderness, cruelty, sensuality and sheer panic. York received a much-deserved Best Actress award at Cannes. The film was not so lucky. Hemdale gave it little publicity and the distributor, Columbia, proved equally unenthusiastic. After three box office disappointments in a row, Altman now needed a commercial property which would at least be given a proper release. George Litto arranged a deal with United Artists for Altman to direct an adaptation of Raymond Chandler's *The Long Goodbye*.

5

The Long Goodbye to Nashville

Returning to the United States in 1972 to work on a film set in Los Angeles, the heart of the American film industry (the opening and closing credits roll to the strains of 'Hooray for Hollywood'), Altman seemed about to embark on a decidedly mainstream career move. His subject matter was a typically hardboiled and cynical Raymond Chandler-Philip Marlowe private eye mystery. The screenplay was by Leigh Brackett, co-author of the much loved Humphrey Bogart-Howard Hawks film version of *The Big Sleep* (1946), a prime example of classical Hollywood film-making. Hawks had been approached by United Artists to direct *The Long Goodbye*, as had Peter Bogdanovich, a specialist in manufactured nostalgia (*The Last Picture Show* (1971), *What's Up Doc?* (1972), *Paper Moon* (1973)). Veteran hard man Lee Marvin was under consideration for the lead role. It is a reflection of Altman's uncertain status in Hollywood that he had been hired to replace original director Brian G. Hutton, best known for his impersonal, straightforward action adventure films (*Where Eagles Dare* (1968), *Kelly's Heroes* (1970)).

All the more surprise then, that *The Long Goodbye* turned out to be as idiosyncratic and individual in its approach as any of Altman's earlier work. In complete contrast to the tough, no-nonsense leading men usually cast as Marlowe (Bogart, Robert Montgomery in *The Lady in the Lake* (1946), George Montgomery in *The Brasher Doubloon* (1947), James Garner in *Marlowe* (1969), Robert Mitchum in *Farewell My Lovely* (1975)), he chose amiable, laid-back Elliott Gould for the starring role (Altman's offbeat casting for the film, including several non-professionals, extends to the smallest bit part and pays off with spot-on performances). The storyline this Marlowe finds himself embroiled in may be more tightly constructed than is usual for Altman's films (the only scenes not directly relevant to the plot are Marlowe's attempts to feed his cat and a bizarre encounter with a heavily-bandaged hospital patient clutching a miniature harmonica), but the familiar concerns with nuances of character; obsessions (notably Marlowe's desire to prove the innocence of a friend accused of murder); eccentricities and the individual's relationship to an absurd, often alien society are present. *The Long Goodbye* also exhibits Altman's remarkably fluid directorial style at its peak. Reunited with cameraman Vilmos Zsigmond (who gives sunny Los Angeles a subdued, unwelcoming look), he employs elaborate, gliding zooms and tracking shots, providing the audience with all the information it needs without resorting to a pedantic picking out of 'significant' actions or details. Dispensing with the fast, relentless pacing typical of many private eye films, Altman lets the events unfold in a more leisurely fashion in keeping with his Marlowe's outwardly laid-back attitude. Marlowe gets the answers he wants, but is quite happy to bide his time. Similarly, while *The Long Goodbye* lacks the violent set-pieces of both the original book and earlier Chandler adaptations (no punch-ups or shoot-outs), it contains moments of brutality far more extreme than anything found in either.

Brackett's script makes a number of changes to Chandler's original story, though the twists and turns of the plot are equally complex. Philip Marlowe receives a visit from his old friend Terry Lennox at three o'clock in the morning. Lennox has had a bad fight with his wife Sylvia and wants to get out of town until things cool down. He asks Marlowe to drive him to Tijuana in Mexico. When Marlowe returns to Los Angeles he is picked up by the police, who inform him that Sylvia Lennox is dead and Terry wanted for her murder. After a few days in custody for refusing to co-operate, Marlowe is suddenly released. Terry Lennox has been found dead in a small-town hotel, with a suicide note confessing to his wife's murder. The police regard the case as closed but Marlowe refuses to believe that his friend was a killer.

Marlowe is hired by Eileen Wade to find her missing husband, the author Roger Wade. He locates Wade, a chronic alcoholic, at a private health clinic run by Dr Verringer. The Wades live on the same private beachfront estate, Malibu Colony, as the Lennoxes but claim to have known them only slightly. Returning to his apartment, Marlowe is hassled by gangster Marty Augustine, who believes that Terry Lennox ran off with money meant for him. Augustine orders Marlowe to return the money. Marlowe follows Augustine to the Wades' house where he argues with Eileen.

A $5,000 bill arrives for Marlowe in the post. With it is a brief goodbye note from Lennox. Marlowe drives to the Mexican town where Lennox's body was found. The authorities show him photographs of the corpse and a death certificate. Marlowe then calls on the Wades to find Roger dead drunk. He asks Eileen Wade about Augustine's visit and her husband's relationship with Sylvia Lennox. As they talk, Roger Wade walks into the sea and drowns. Distraught, Eileen confesses to Marlowe that Roger and Sylvia were lovers. She believes that her husband murdered Sylvia Lennox and paid Dr Verringer for an alibi.

Augustine's money reappears. Eileen Wade leaves town, putting her house up for sale. Marlowe drives back to the scene of Terry Lennox's death and offers the local police $5,000 to tell him what really happened to his late friend. He walks to a large house on the outskirts of the town to find Lennox alive and well. Lennox readily admits to killing his wife and faking his own death. Sylvia had discovered his affair with Eileen Wade and was going to tell the police about his dealings with Augustine. Marlowe shoots Lennox dead. On his way out of town he passes Eileen Wade. Marlowe walks straight on.

Updated from the early fifties (Chandler's book was published in 1953) to the present day, *The Long Goodbye* is a study of a moral and decent man cast adrift in a selfish, self-obsessed society where lives can be thrown away without a backward glance and any notions of friendship or loyalty are meaningless. As portrayed by Elliott Gould, Marlowe is a seemingly easy-going, slightly naive man whose credo is 'it's okay with me'. Dressed in a crumpled dark suit and driving a car at least twenty years old, this Philip Marlowe is a character out of time. His values are those of another, more honourable (not to say mythical) age. He sticks by his worthless 'friend' despite intimidation from the police ('Marlowe with an 'e'. That sounds like a fag name') and Lennox's crooked associates. He is deceived and used by Eileen Wade, an action made worse by her overtures of friendship. Even the spaced-out female hippies living in the apartment next to his seem aware of his existence only when they want a favour.

Altman made his intentions clear when *The Long Goodbye* was released, 'Chandler used Marlowe to comment on his own time, so I thought it would be an engaging exercise to use him to comment on our present age.' Philip Marlowe has been asleep for twenty years, waking up to find a world turned sour, a harder, more cynical age. The noble (if unkempt) private eye is now a hopeless anachronism. Either reviewers could not comprehend this notion or they just didn't want to know. Charles Champlin dismissed Gould's Marlowe as 'an untidy, unshaven, semi-literate dimwit slob who could not locate a missing skyscraper'. Michael Billington saw the whole film as 'a spit in the eye to a great writer'. *Sight and Sound* seemed to latch on to Altman's ideas, but looked on the resulting work as a self-defeating exercise, 'Altman's fragmentation bomb blows up itself rather than the myths he has said he wants to lay to rest.'

Our first glimpse of Marlowe is certainly less than flattering. Sprawled on his bed in the early hours of the morning, fast asleep but fully-dressed, he is rudely awoken by the mewing and trampling of his hungry cat. Still half asleep, Marlowe prepares food for the cat and, when it refuses to eat it, drives over to a 24-hour supermarket to purchase the cat's favourite brand of pet food. The man has the air of an amiable slob for whom no favour is too much trouble. Lennox's unusual request to be driven two hundred miles over the Mexican border arouses no great surprise or suspicion. As the story progresses, however, a sharper, more canny Marlowe becomes apparent. He lets the police shove him around a little but refuses to answer questions unless they follow proper procedure. When Eileen Wade contacts him he specifies straight away that he won't do divorce work and asks for $50 a day plus expenses (the only private eye clichés spoken by Marlowe in the entire film). Roger Wade is efficiently and quickly located at Verringer's clinic, despite the denials of the staff that he's ever been there. After Augustine's first visit, Marlowe easily shakes the tail put on him by the gangster and follows Augustine to his meeting with Eileen. Marlowe's only blind spot in the film is Terry Lennox (ex-baseball player Jim Bouton). We learn little of the nature of their friendship (Marlowe will only say that they've known each other 'a long time'), but it quickly becomes apparent that Marlowe knows next to nothing about Lennox's dubious business dealings and even more dubious private life. He refutes a policeman's description of Lennox as 'a gambler and a hood' and will not listen to any suggestion (be it from the police or Augustine) that Terry murdered his wife. For Marlowe, friendship and the loyalty that (for him) friendship demands are everything. It is Lennox's betrayal of this ideal, rather than police insults or a mobster's punch in the stomach, that finally drives Marlowe to anger and a lethal demonstration of his toughness.

Lennox's casual amorality is, of course, symptomatic of the society he moves in. Writers, gangsters, society hostesses and bogus doctors mix freely and easily because everyone is out to grab what they can for themselves and a friendship or deal can be made or broken in an instant. Eileen Wade (coolly played by Nina Van Pallandt, formerly one half of the sixties singing duo, Nina and Frederick) seems a genuinely warm and devoted wife, nobly bearing the bruises inflicted by a drunken, self-pitying husband, but all the time she has been carrying on an affair with Terry Lennox. She lets Marlowe discover the 'truth' about Roger and Sylvia Lennox, knowing full well that he would rather believe her husband to be a murderer than accept Terry's guilt. (In Chandler's novel, it is Eileen who murders Sylvia Lennox. She then kills Roger Wade because he knows of her crime and, finally, kills herself with an overdose.) Eileen's mild flirtation with Marlowe ('I feel you're a man I can trust'), treating him to a candle-lit dinner for two, shows how far she is prepared to go to hide Lennox's and her own guilt.

Eileen Wade represents callous, unfeeling deception at its most chic. Marty Augustine (film director Mark Rydell) is at least open about his aims and intentions. Lennox stole his money and he wants it back (Sylvia's murder is for him only a minor misdemeanour). His chief gripe with Marlowe on their first meeting is the fact that he's missing Friday attendance at Temple. Both a good Jew and an equal opportunities employer (his hoods include a Mexican, an Italian and an Irishman, not to mention a young Austrian named Arnold Schwarzenegger), Augustine sees himself as a model wealthy citizen, with a wife, three children, tennis lessons three times a week and a house full of servants. Marlowe may get slugged for making a 'smart crack', but otherwise Augustine does not appear interested in hurting him (unlike Menendez, the equivalent character in the book, who has Marlowe pistol-whipped for interfering in his business), even telling his men to be careful when they search Marlowe's apartment for the missing money. That said, Augustine provides the most disturbing moment in the film, smashing a Coke bottle across his placid girlfriend's face (an act which would appal Menendez, who plays his thuggery by the book) to make Marlowe appreciate that he means business ('That's someone I love. You I don't even like'). Augustine's insecurity about his status as a 'big' man (he constantly accuses Marlowe of making jokes at his expense) manifests itself in misdirected brutality and an eccentric literal-mindedness, as when he tells Marlowe to take his clothes off to prove that he has nothing to hide. If, ultimately, Augustine seems marginally less repellent than Lennox and Eileen Wade, it is because he takes only what belongs to him. Once the money is returned, he has no further interest in Marlowe. More importantly, he takes no part in the sordid cover-up of Sylvia Lennox's murder.

If Marlowe encounters anyone remotely resembling a kindred spirit in *The Long Goodbye*, it is Harry (David Arkin), one of Augustine's men. Dressed like a parody of a gangster, in a black suit, black shirt and white tie, Harry yearns for the old days ('I can remember when people just had jobs') and cites George Raft as his role model. Unlike Marlowe, Harry is not up to the demands of his job. Marlowe has to let him know where he's going so he won't have too much difficulty tailing him. When Augustine orders Harry to cut Marlowe with a switchblade, he is genuinely horrified. As Marlowe notes with a sigh, he will 'never be a first grade hood'. The only other character to yearn for times gone by is Roger Wade (forcefully played by the imposing Sterling Hayden, who replaced *Bonanza* star Dan Blocker in the role when the latter died suddenly), who seems to despise the people he mixes with at his wife's beach parties and urges her to remember the good things in their life together. Marlowe enjoys a drinking session with Wade (much of the dialogue in this scene was improvised by Gould and Hayden) but the latter is too far gone in his drunken despair. Impotent

both as a writer and a husband (and well aware of his wife's adultery), Wade blusters and rants at the leech-like Dr Verringer (a man closely resembling a malicious pixie), only to give in to him after being slapped round the face like a difficult child. Wade is easily the most pathetic character in *The Long Goodbye*. Unable to live up to his own ideal of true manliness, he takes petty revenge on his wife by informing Sylvia Lennox of Eileen's affair with Terry. Thus he is partly responsible for her death, setting in motion the chain of events that Marlowe must finally bring to a bitter conclusion. Perhaps it is this knowledge of his part in Sylvia's murder, as much as his own personal despair, which leads Roger Wade to his watery suicide.

Wade provides Sylvia Lennox with the information that leads (albeit indirectly) to her death. Terry Lennox precipitates his own downfall through his contemptible attempt at squaring things with Marlowe (a feeble apology and a cash bribe). Marlowe uses the $5,000 sent by Lennox (which incidentally was not Lennox's to give, being part of the payment he stole from Augustine) to 'persuade' the Mexican authorities to give him a true account of their dealings with Lennox. Marlowe's anger is directed entirely at his former friend. He appears impressed rather than angered at the Mexicans' elaborate deception ('You told me a good story and I saw some pretty good pictures'). Lennox has deceived and used Marlowe from the beginning. He even put on gloves before calling on his friend for the ride to Tijuana, so only the bruises on his face (presumably the result of Sylvia's attempts to defend herself) would show, not the marks left on his knuckles as a result of beating his wife to death. We do not see the pictures of Sylvia's corpse that the police show Marlowe, but it is made clear that her head was reduced to a bloody pulp. Lennox is as casual about his wife's murder ('I had to kill her, I had no choice'), as he is about betraying Marlowe's trust ('What are friends for?') (The Lennox of the book may be what Chandler terms a 'moral defeatist' but he is no vicious killer; weak and unprincipled, Chandler's Lennox is a sad, pitiful man.) This 'so what?' attitude – reflecting a nasty amorality – is contrasted with Marlowe's deceptively casual air. When the time comes, Marlowe will always stand for what he believes to be right. Lennox's complete inability to comprehend this (he cannot understand why Marlowe will not have a drink with him) illustrates all too clearly the vast moral gulf dividing them:

LENNOX: What the hell. Nobody cares.
MARLOWE: Yeah, nobody cares but me.

The Long Goodbye – Philip Marlowe (Elliott Gould) and his cat

LENNOX: Well, that's you Marlowe. You'll never learn. You're a born loser.

MARLOWE: Yeah, I even lost my cat.

Up until this point, we did not know if Marlowe even possessed a gun, let alone the ability to shoot one (just as McCabe's skills as a gunfighter were not revealed until he needed them). His killing of Lennox, performed with the cold efficiency of a man who has had to kill before, was condemned by some as a complete betrayal of Chandler's character: the knight in tarnished armour transformed into a cold-blooded murderer. Others misread the action as the result of the corrupting influence of the decadent society now surrounding Marlowe. It makes more sense to regard the shooting of Lennox as the ultimate expression of Marlowe's code of honour. Lennox is both a traitor (to his friendship with Marlowe) and a brutal murderer. The law cannot touch him (he is legally dead) so it is up to Marlowe to see justice done and execute the guilty man. As Altman himself pointed out, there can be no doubt that the killing is morally justified. Marlowe will face no legal retribution for his act (a man cannot be killed twice), and while Eileen Wade is free from the law's grasp, she has lost everything she strived for. Her Mexican paradise with Terry Lennox will now never be.

The Long Goodbye ends with Marlowe walking down a tree-lined avenue to an ironic reprise of 'Hooray for Hollywood'. There is nothing to cheer about in the Hollywood Altman has just shown us. All the references to the movie industry – present throughout the film but kept fairly peripheral – look back to the golden age: the security man at the Malibu Colony does impersonations of Barbara Stanwyck, James Stewart, Cary Grant and Walter Brennan; Marlowe smears fingerprint ink over his face and does an impromptu Al Jolson; when the police refuse to listen to Eileen Wade's version of events Marlowe threatens to bring in Ronald Reagan (at the time State Governor of California). More pertinent to the present is the John Williams/Johnny Mercer theme song, also called 'The Long Goodbye'. This is played over the onscreen events in several versions (ranging from piano solo to Spanish guitar and castanets) and often becomes a part of the film's fabric: Marlowe sings a few lines, the supermarket plays a dreadful 'muzak' version, a bar pianist attempts to learn the tune from scratch. Marlowe first says goodbye to Terry Lennox in Tijuana in the film's opening sequence, still believing the latter to be a good friend worth taking trouble for. Lennox attempts another farewell in his note sent with the $5,000 bill. Marlowe, however, cannot say a proper goodbye to his old friend until he knows the truth about him (as a promotional slogan for the film rather crudely put it: 'Nothing says goodbye like a bullet'). We assume that Marlowe is heading back to Los Angeles as the screen fades to black, but in a way his destination is not important. A man out of his time wherever he goes, Marlowe will always be more than equal to the schemings of the morally bankrupt world that surrounds him.

It is worth dwelling at length on *The Long Goodbye* as it stands as a near perfect example of Altman's ability to rework the familiar elements of a well-worn genre into a highly personal piece of film-making (he was attracted to Brackett's script by the idea of Marlowe killing his best friend, a major departure from the book). Genre purists did not care for this near 'blasphemous' revision, as Altman discovered to his cost. Unfavourable reviews and poor box office returns led to the film being abruptly withdrawn from release. In desperation, United Artists devised a new publicity campaign, promoting *The Long Goodbye* as an outright parody (many critics certainly looked on it as a travesty). This re-release proved no more successful.

Despite *The Long Goodbye*'s disastrous reception, Altman and George Litto managed to convince United Artists to back the director's next film, *Thieves Like Us* (Litto served as executive producer on the film, which suggests some agreement with United Artists to keep a close eye on his erring client). Based on a 1937 novel by Edward Anderson, this Depression-era tale of bank robbers, betrayal and doomed romance had been a pet project of Altman's for a number of years. The early seventies mini-vogue for period rural gangster movies (such as Roger Corman's *Bloody Mama* (1970), Robert Aldrich's *The Grissom Gang* (1971), Martin Scorsese's *Boxcar Bertha* (1972) and John Milius' *Dillinger* (1973)) gave the idea a certain commercial attraction, Nicholas Ray's *They Live by Night* (1948) had also used Anderson's book as its source material, though both Altman and screenwriter Joan Tewkesbury claim not to have seen this earlier version.

Tewkesbury, a respected writer/director from the theatre, was one of several production personnel working with Altman for the first time in key positions (Tewkesbury had served as a lowly script supervisor on *McCabe and Mrs Miller*). Others included cameraman Jean Boffety (Vilmos Zsigmond's price tag was now too high for Altman's medium budgets) and costume designer Scott Bushnell, who would continue to work for Altman both in this capacity (most notably for *Popeye* and *Vincent and Theo*) and as an associate producer (location manager). The script for *Thieves Like Us* is credited to Calder Willingham, Tewkesbury and Altman, which is (by all accounts) slightly misleading. Willingham (who co-scripted Marlon Brando's psychological western, *One Eyed Jacks* (1961), and *The Graduate* (1967)) wrote a first draft screenplay. Tewkesbury disregarded this in favour of working directly from the book. Altman, anxious to retain the flavour of Anderson's original, made very few changes to her script.

The leading roles of tragic lovers Bowie and Keechie were given to Keith Carradine and Shelley Duvall, who both contribute likeable, touching performances. Bowie, convicted of murder (in self-defence; he is not a hardened criminal), is serving his sentence as part of a Southern chain gang. Along with two other prisoners, T-Dub (Bert Remsen) and Chicamaw Mobley (John Schuck), he manages to escape and the three of them take to robbing banks. They are not the most competent of thieves, however (the only robbery shown in detail is a disaster), and soon have to seek refuge from the police with Chicamaw's storekeeper brother Dee (Tom Skerritt) and his daughter Keechie. Bowie and Keechie fall in love, but the police, aided by the treachery of the thieves' friends and their own mistakes, are closing in.

Bowie's relationship with Keechie is in marked contrast to his slightly uneasy partnership with his fellow thieves. T-Dub and Chicamaw have little to offer him other than transient notoriety and an empty sense of camaraderie. Keechie, who tends to Bowie's wounds after a car crash, offers at least a chance of love and a different way of life. Inevitably, Bowie is torn between his 'obligation' to his partners (though he abandons Chicamaw after the latter needlessly kills a hostage) and Keechie's wish for him to turn his back on crime.

Thieves Like Us reaches its sad denouement with Bowie's death at the hands of machinegun-happy state troopers. Here the film makes its one significant departure from the book by sparing Keechie from the same fate (though she is forced to look on as her lover is killed). Altman justified this change by arguing that while the thieves are fated to end their less than brilliant careers either in prison (like Chicamaw) or dead (like Bowie and T-Dub), the women who support and shelter them survive, albeit disillusioned and embittered. Keechie will in time become like Mattie (Louise Fletcher), T-Dub's sister-in-law, who agrees to give the thieves shelter before (by implication at least) betraying Bowie to the police. United Artists agreed to the new ending (which in its way is as pessimistic as the original, as well as lacking the element of romantic tragedy) on the more practical grounds that the book's climax was too similar to *Bonnie and Clyde*. The film ends with a wistful coda, as Keechie, pregnant with Bowie's child, leaves the scene of her lover's death to seek a new life elsewhere. Boarding a train, she becomes just another figure in the milling crowd, disappearing into anonymity.

The period setting of *Thieves Like Us* is beautifully captured (Altman, of course, grew up during the Depression, though his own family was relatively unscathed by economic disaster), with careful attention paid to backgrounds, props and costumes. Determined to be as authentic as possible, Altman hired a special visual consultant, Jack DeGovia. The film also

Thieves Like Us – Bowie (Keith Carradine) and Keechie (Shelley Duvall)

makes effective use of thirties radio broadcasts (period songs take the place of the usual musical score), adding an extra dimension to the world the characters move in. The radio programmes also serve as commentary on the main action. When Bowie and Keechie make love, a dramatization of *Romeo and Juliet* is heard in the background (another of Altman's additions to the script). This can be read as either reinforcing the idea of a pure love doomed by fate (McGilligan) or merely a touch of cruel irony (Geoff Andrew). There is certainly no place for tender romance in the drab, hostile world inhabited by Bowie and Keechie.

This downbeat tone made *Thieves Like Us* something of a hard sell for United Artists, especially as its leisurely pace did not allow for the fast and furious action sequences usually associated with the crime drama. The film followed the by now almost standard Altman pattern of critical praise, limited release and minimal box office.

Had the management at Metro Goldwyn Mayer been a little more reasonable, Altman's subsequent film, *California Split* (1974), would have been the motion picture debut of director Steven Spielberg. The script, by actor turned writer Joseph Walsh, attracted the studio's interest, as did Spielberg's success with the television movie *Duel* (1971). Neither Walsh nor Spielberg, however, were happy with the changes MGM wanted made to Walsh's tale of seedy gamblers in pursuit of a big win and the project stalled. Litto obtained the script for Altman, and arranged a production deal with Columbia. (Spielberg, in the meantime, finally broke in feature films with *The Sugarland Express* (1974)).

Walsh intended *California Split* as a 'celebration' of gambling which eventually turns sour. The excitement felt by the main characters, Bill (George Segal) and Charlie (Elliott Gould), as they play for large stakes, is

California Split – Bill (George Segal) and Charlie (Elliott Gould)

merely a symptom of an unhealthy obsession (or addiction) which blocks out all other concerns. After a chance meeting at a casino bar (as Kolker says, the whole film is structured like one long game of chance), the two men become friends ('buddies') on the strictly temporary basis of a mutual desire for a lucky streak. Their escapades unfold in an episodic fashion, with the more impulsive Charlie leading, Bill tagging behind. Two prostitute friends of Charlie, Barbara (Ann Prentiss) and Susan (Gwen Welles), provide the men with refuge from the casinos and their various misfortunes. Bill does eventually enjoy an impressive win in Reno, only to find he no longer experiences the thrill of the true gambler.

California Split proved to be a suitable vehicle for Altman's style (the director had more than a passing interest in gambling, a passion inherited from his father), but he found himself in conflict with Walsh. Acting as the film's producer as well as its writer (he also appears in a supporting role), Walsh was in a position to protect his vision of the film and resisted any significant changes in the script. As a compromise, he agreed to Altman improvising with the background figures. This may account (in part at least) for the greater than usual emphasis on the supporting characters and extras, with their dialogue often dominating the soundtrack (a number of the extras used were members of an organization for ex-addicts who simply made up their own lines; this added a further touch of realism to the film but did not go down well with the Extras Guild). Altman also employs an onscreen link, in this case a casino singer (Phyllis Shotwell), to comment on the proceedings.

While *California Split* contains much of interest, it is a difficult film to appreciate for viewers not drawn to the world it lays bare in such unrelenting detail. The often murky visuals and messy soundtrack, while in keeping with the overall style, can become wearying. Bill and Charlie's behaviour, their gambling fixation aside, is as liable to irritate as arouse sympathy. An unkind trick played on one of Barbara and Susan's customers (a transvestite) recalls the cruel humiliation of Hotlips in *M*A*S*H*. That said, *California Split* turned out to be a modest financial success, comfortably recovering its costs. The film also marked Altman's last collaboration with his longtime editor Lou Lombardo, who departed to become a director in his own right with the competent espionage thriller *Russian Roulette* (1975), a middling vehicle for George Segal (his son, Tony Lombardo, an assistant editor on *Thieves Like Us* and *California Split*, remained with Altman, eventually graduating to editor with *A Wedding*).

During the production of *California Split*, Altman set writer Joan Tewkesbury to work on the screenplay for his next film, *Nashville*, a darkly satirical look at contemporary American Society. The deal with United

Artists which produced *Thieves Like Us* involved a second picture, a country-and-western musical called *The Great Southern Amusement Company*. Altman liked the idea but not the script and offered *Nashville* as an alternative. While United Artists deliberated over financing the film, George Litto, Altman's longtime agent and *Nashville*'s intended producer, expressed strong reservations about the project (chiefly the violent ending and Altman's decision to have his actors write their own songs) and quit. This did little to reassure the already dubious United Artists executives and they refused to guarantee any backing. *Nashville* was rescued from oblivion by the ABC company, which provided the modest budget (under $3 million) on the grounds that its record division could market the soundtrack album.

Joan Tewkesbury's script for *Nashville* derived from research carried out during a short stay in the country-and-western capital (in the state of Tennessee). The multi-faceted storyline takes place over a long weekend as various singing stars gather to record new material and perform live in clubs, churches, on boats and at the Grand Ole Opry. Along with the celebrities, we have their assorted friends, relatives and business associates plus a number of hopefuls looking for their big breaks. Into this showbusiness milieu, Tewkesbury injects a strong political dimension in the form of the election campaign for independent presidential candidate Hal Philip Walker and his Replacement Party. With the Watergate scandal still fresh in the public mind (Tewkesbury completed the *Nashville* scripts in 1974), Altman wanted to comment on politics and politicians and *Nashville* is very consciously a film about leadership, politics, celebrity and showbusiness (and the differences, if any, between them). It is a measure of the film's success that it makes its points without collapsing under the weight of its ambition or any sense of self-importance.

From its pre-credits sequence, which announces the 24 'star' actors (though a fair number play brief, if colourful, bit parts) in the style of an especially awful advert for a 'Best of . . .' country-and-western album, to the closing tilt up to the sky as the camera abandons these same sad people on the stage below, *Nashville* carefully interweaves both its themes and its characters in a mosaic-style structure. The first shot introduces the Hal Philip Walker campaign van, delivering the candidate's political platform via loudspeaker announcements ('Fellow taxpayers and stockholders of America'), which reappears on the edges of scenes throughout the film (and also serves as a typical Altman link/punctuation). We are then introduced to the first of the singing stars as Haven Hamilton (Henry Gibson) attempts to record the mock-patriotic '200 Years' ('We must be doing something right to last 200 years'), only to be distracted by Opal (Geraldine Chaplin), a BBC journalist who pesters various characters with inane questions and delivers rambling, pretentious monologues about nothing at all.

Adorned with a ridiculous toupee, Haven Hamilton sings about loyalty, patriotism and family ('For the sake of the children, I must say goodbye'), but never comes across as anything more than an old pro raking in the cash. This is a man who has raised insincerity into an art form. By contrast, Barbara Jean (Ronee Blakley), the top female star, seems almost painfully sincere. After her arrival at Nashville's airport (a major media event), she collapses and spends much of the film in a hospital room, where we glimpse both the loneliness of her existence and her total subservience to Barnett (Allen Garfield), her domineering husband/manager. Many of her songs express a heartfelt nostalgia for childhood and family life, though it is made clear that her mother pushed her into a singing career at a very young age. Barbara Jean has always been manipulated and exploited.

Connie White (Karen Black), Barbara Jean's arch rival, projects the same phoney warmth and friendliness as Haven Hamilton (in Barnett's view, all his wife's fellow singers are 'phonies'). Although the character is little more than a cameo role (one of Altman's additions to the script), she provides one of the film's most telling moments. Barnett offers her a gift as a token of thanks after she stands in for Barbara Jean at the Grand Ole Opry concert. Connie White thanks him but never takes the gift. This way, she keeps Barbara Jean in her debt (an uncomfortable position) and also humiliates Barnett in front of the onlookers (including Haven Hamilton). One of the bleakest aspects of *Nashville* is its assertion that the Whites and Hamiltons of the showbusiness world will flourish, while those like Barbara Jean are too vulnerable to survive.

Tommy Brown (Timothy Brown), a black country-and-western singer, seems to be accepted by the white stars, though the film's other black character, Wade (Robert Doqui), accuses him of being a traitor to his people ('the whitest nigger in town'). Of the non-country stars, the most intriguing is Tom Frank (Keith Carradine), part of the folk trio Tom, Bill (Allan Nicholls) and Mary (Christina Raines). Blessed with an easy-going charm, Tom enjoys sexual liaisons with Opal; Mary (Bill's wife); Linnea Reese (Lily Tomlin), an amateur gospel singer and wife of the local attorney, and LA Joan (Shelley Duvall), an empty-headed groupie who changes her appearance as frequently as she changes boyfriends. His unwillingness (perhaps inability) to express any affection for the various women in his life (he will not respond to any declaration of love, at one point coolly playing with Linnea Reese's infatuation while simultaneously taking a 'phone call from another lovesick girlfriend) reflects an almost universal lack of basic human feeling among *Nashville's* characters. Several arouse our passing sympathy: Barbara Jean; Bud Hamilton (Dave Peel), Haven Hamilton's amiable son and business manager; Mr Green (Keenan

Wynn), the only 'normal' (i.e. not connected to the music business) Nashville resident, whose concern over his sick wife holds no great importance for anyone else. Any expression of honest emotion, however, is shown to result only in indifference, humiliation or embarrassment. Tom also supplies *Nashville*'s anthem, 'It Don't Worry Me' (written by Carradine), a song repeated several times during the film. As Kolker says, the lyrics express the essential passivity common to all the characters (there are no Altman heroes in this film). Walker's pronouncement that it is up to the ordinary people to change America ('balance the books') falls on disinterested ears.

Nashville's political thread is effectively embodied in the character of John Triplette (Michael Murphy), campaign manager for Hal Philip Walker (Walker himself is seen only once in a brief long shot). On the lookout for celebrities to endorse Walker at his Tennessee rally, Triplette sets about recruiting singing stars as the usual movie stars are just too weird for the 'grass roots' crowd (two film stars who do appear, Julie Christie and Elliott Gould, go largely unrecognized). His task is depressingly straightforward. Haven Hamilton initially declines on the grounds that he will not publicly support any political candidate, but is swayed by the offer of a chance to become a State Governor. Bill accepts (on behalf of himself, Tom and Mary) as he doesn't care about politics either way and looks on the event as a good publicity opportunity. Even when faced with Barnett's steadfast refusal to let his wife appear with Walker, Triplette gets lucky. Barabara Jean falters during a public concert (unstable throughout the film, she seems on the verge of a nervous collapse), and Barnett is forced to placate the hostile audience by promising that she will perform for free at the Walker rally. Triplette's contempt for these people ('local yokels') is expressed more than once. In one of the film's grimmest moments, he talks a tone-deaf amateur singer, Sueleen Gay (Gwen Welles), into performing a striptease at a fundraising event for local businessmen (an act of misogynist exploitation which the film explicitly condemns). Her 'reward' is a chance to make a bigger fool of herself singing at the rally.

Nashville's finale sees all the main characters brought together for the first time (though a chaotic but non-fatal freeway pile-up after the airport scene involves everyone apart from Barbara Jean and Barnett). As the stars line up to perform for Walker in front of the city's Parthenon building (a piece of pseudo-classical architecture dating back to the thirties), a gigantic Stars and Stripes hanging above them, all Triplette's machinations appear to have paid off. Barbara Jean sings wistfully about 'Mom and Dad' to rapturous applause. Chaos arrives in the form of a demented gunman, Kenny (David Hayward), who shoots both Barbara Jean and Haven Hamilton, killing one and wounding the other. This shock ending, included by Altman

Nashville – Barbara Jean (Ronee Blakley) and Haven Hamilton (Henry Gibson)

against Tewkesbury's wishes, can seem both abrupt and unmotivated but there are a number of clues planted in earlier scenes. When we first see Barbara Jean, she is wearing a long white dress similar to the traditional robe worn by a sacrificial victim. Shortly after, she faints dead away (Ronee Blakley's fragile appearance underlines her character's victim status). There is talk of assassinations, especially the Kennedy murder and the accompanying conspiracy theories. Kenny himself is one of the film's most marginal figures. A telephone conversation reveals a troubled relationship with his mother, otherwise he is characterized only by his overly 'straight' appearance (neither a hippy nor a 'good ole boy') and his ever present instrument case, which remains unopened until the shooting starts.

Altman's refusal to provide any strong motivation for Kenny's action (he argues that it is up to the individual viewer to decide why he kills Barbara Jean; there is no definite, definitive explanation) underlines the arbitrary nature of violence (did Kenny intend to shoot Haven Hamilton as well?) and the futility of looking for reasons why (so much for conspiracy theories).

Filmed by Altman in a near-documentary style (many of the musical sequences could pass for the genuine article), *Nashville* remains a scathing commentary on modern America. This is as soulless a world as that depicted in *The Long Goodbye*, one where anything (or anyone) can be bought and sold, so long as it is attractively packaged. The empty slogans and myths peddled by politicians and singers alike go unquestioned and unchallenged (as the song puts it: 'You may say that I ain't free, It don't worry me'). *Nashville* employs a directness of approach which may surprise those used to its director's more playful, offbeat or downright strange films (as McGilligan notes, Altman rarely includes topical references in his films). There is a sense of anger and frustration to the film largely absent from his later 'state of the nation' satires, *A Wedding* and *Health*. The bleakest moment in *Nashville* is not the death of Barbara Jean but its immediate aftermath. As the assembled crowd falls into confusion, Haven Hamilton (whose attempt to shield Barbara Jean is his one act of genuine selflessness) calls for someone to sing ('This isn't Dallas'). A young unknown named Albuquerque (Barbara Harris) picks up Barbara Jean's fallen microphone and nervously sings the first lines of 'It Don't Worry Me'. As the crowd join in, she gains confidence, eventually delivering a 'star' performance while the song disperses the panic as effectively as any sedative. Order is restored and Barbara Jean is replaced by a new singing star (who, incidentally, first strolled into Nashville with Kenny at her side). Nothing changes except the faces on the album covers.

Released in 1975 to critical acclaim, *Nashville* had the potential to be a hit on the scale of *M*A*S*H*. Unfortunately, its distributor, Paramount, decided that the film was an 'art' movie rather than popular fare. *Nashville* grossed $10 million in domestic rentals, ensuring a respectable profit, but failed to received the wide release necessary for big box-office returns. The film received five Academy Award nominations (including Best Film and Best Director), only to see *One Flew Over the Cuckoo's Nest* (1975) win in all the major categories (though *Nashville* took the award for Best Original Song, Keith Carradine's 'I'm Easy'). Halfway through the most productive phase of his career, Altman had come tantalizingly close to re-establishing himself as a commercial director. In the event, *Nashville* attracted enough acclaim to place Altman in good standing with the big studios. His career was still in good health.

6

Three Women and a Sailor

Altman's new-found favour with the major studios created a certain amount of interest in various projects but no firm production deals. Two sport-related films based on best-selling books, *Eight Men Out* (filmed by John Sayles in 1988) and *North Dallas Forty* (filmed by Ted Kotcheff in 1979) came to nothing. *Yigepoxy* (also known as *Easy and Hard Ways Out*), a military black comedy in the *M*A*S*H* mould, attracted both a backer (Warner) and stars (Peter Falk and Sterling Hayden) before suffering an indefinite postponement. Warner wanted rewrites and cast changes that Altman was not prepared to make. This left two other literary properties, Kurt Vonnegut's *Breakfast of Champions* and E.L. Doctorow's epic *Ragtime*. The rights to the Vonnegut book had not yet been secured, so *Ragtime* seemed the more viable project. All Altman needed was a deal with the owner of the film rights, producer/mogul Dino de Laurentiis.

Best known for his populist, comic-strip films (*Barbarella* (1968), *King Kong* (1976), *Flash Gordon* (1980), *Conan the Barbarian* (1982)), de Laurentiis also had a respectable track record as a producer of more thoughtful works (including Federico Fellini's *La Strada* (1954)). Altman's ambitious ideas for *Ragtime* (to be scripted by Joan Tewkesbury) aroused his interest. Rather than embark on this extremely expensive film straight away, however, de Laurentiis offered the director another of his upmarket properties, Arthur Kopit's surreal play *Indians*. Unenthusiastic, Altman initially turned it down, but with no other projects ready to go into production and the chance to make *Ragtime* if this film went smoothly, he finally agreed. Armed with his highest budget so far ($6 million) and an impressive cast headed by Paul Newman and Burt Lancaster, Altman set about making a film that deflated the myths of the old American West (though it is in no practical sense a western). The result, *Buffalo Bill and the Indians, or Sitting Bull's History Lesson*, is a dull disappointment, a failed attempt to add a note of subversion to the patriotic celebrations of America's Bicentennial year (1976). Little of Kopit's original survives (Altman claimed never to have seen *Indians* performed or even read the text all the way through) and the shift in emphasis from the Native American to the treacherous White Man misfires.

Unlike the later *Vincent and Theo*, there is little of the biopic about *Buffalo Bill and the Indians*. The setting, 'Buffalo' Bill Cody's Wild West Show during one of its winter camps, is merely a platform for a series of sketches on the themes of popular history ('How the West was Won'), revealed to be nothing more than elaborate lies, and celebrity, seen here as entirely manufactured. The minimal plot involves Bill (Newman) recruiting the elderly Sitting Bull (Frank Kaquitts) as one of his 'stars'. Concerned only with trying to improve the desperate situation of his people, Sitting Bull has no time for Bill's rewriting of the past through his show. Having failed to persuade the President, Grover Cleveland, to listen to his pleas, he departs into the wilderness.

The Wild West Show is a drab, shabby affair (though the historical Buffalo Bill added a touch of exoticism by employing Russian Cossack riders and Japanese Samurai), with unimpressive 'Indian raids', trick riding and sharpshooting. Nevertheless, audiences love it, as this is the way they want the West to have been. Only one performer, 'sureshot' Annie Oakley, shows any respect or friendliness towards the Indians (she even threatens to quit the show when Bill decides to fire Sitting Bull). The others comply with their leader's patronizing, insulting attitude.

Buffalo Bill is an inversion of Altman's real heroes, such as McCabe, Marlowe and Popeye. These people may seem bumbling, incompetent and decidedly unheroic, but prove themselves when tested. Bill is a 'hero' only on the surface, carefully groomed for stardom. Underneath he is weak and feeble (his pathetic ranting recalls Roger Wade in *The Long Goodbye*). Alcoholic, impotent and vain, he restages his greatest 'triumphs' as a scout and Indian fighter, but outside the show draws his guns only to shoot at a canary belonging to his mistress ('I hate birds'). The other members of the Wild West Show treat Bill as if he was his own character. Ned Buntline (Lancaster), the dime novelist who created Buffalo Bill out of William Frederick Cody, recognizes that his creation has taken on a life of its own. He no longer has any part in Bill's success and eventually departs from the camp.

Sitting Bull, though old, tired and ill, retains his dignity and his integrity. Bill seeks to exploit and humiliate him, transforming the Indian leader into a stereotyped 'savage', but he will not become a part of Bill's fantasy world ('Codyland'). The film's ending is downbeat. Sitting Bull is murdered soon after he leaves the Wild West Show. Bill carries on with his act, employing the chief's interpreter (Will Sampson) to play the dead Indian in a feebly staged 'duel to the death' act.

The essence of the film is summed up by its slightly awkward title. *Buffalo Bill and the Indians* could be a traditional western, with a heroic pioneer battling dangerous natives. This is the story (or myth) the Wild West Show sells its audience. The subtitle, *Sitting Bull's History Lesson*, is ambiguous – is Sitting Bull giving or taking the lesson? The Indian has a story to tell but calls history an 'insult to the dead'. Certainly, Bill's idea of

Buffalo Bill and the Indians – 'Buffalo' Bill Cody (Paul Newman) holds court

history, reinvented to suit his own personal myth, is an insult. Yet it has become accepted as fact, legend being much more potent (and palatable) than the shameful truth of broken promises and treaties. This is the lesson Sitting Bull must learn before realizing that he is on a hopeless mission (the historical Sitting Bull summed up his people's situation with grim brevity: 'The Indians must keep quiet or die').

As an intellectual debate, *Buffalo Bill and the Indians* is not without interest. It has a valid, if not particularly original point to make about popular history, though *Nashville* had already given the concept of celebrity a thorough going-over on the satirical rack and this film has little to add. As drama or character study it is a non-starter. The strong cast, which includes Harvey Keitel, Geraldine Chaplin, Joel Grey, Kevin McCarthy and Shelley Duvall, is largely wasted as the supporting characters – producers, agents, writers, performers and relatives all living off Bill's celebrity – are little more than ciphers. The two Indians are sympathetic without being properly developed as people (possibly because the white characters regard them as alien and incomprehensible). Burt Lancaster is restricted to a cameo role and even Paul Newman's performance seems curiously underpowered. The film is further doomed by its drab visual style and a lack of the lively quirkiness present in Altman's best work.

During post-production on *Buffalo Bill and the Indians*, Dino de Laurentiis ordered Altman to speed up the editing to meet the preview deadline (McGilligan suggests that this haste hurt the film, though it is difficult to see how it could have been radically improved). Lukewarm reviews confirmed de Laurentiis' lack of faith in the end product and, after negligible distribution in the United States (through United Artists), the film was cut by around twenty minutes before being released overseas. Altman also lost his chance to make *Ragtime*. De Laurentiis gave the film to *One Flew Over the Cuckoo's Nest* director Milos Forman (released in 1981, *Ragtime* proved a critical disappointment and a commercial disaster). To make matters worse, Warner finally rejected *Yigepoxy* and Altman failed to win the rights to *Breakfast of Champions*. The opportunities created by *Nashville* had evaporated almost as soon as they arose.

Having suffered a string of aborted projects and a resounding box-office failure Altman found a sympathetic patron in the form of Alan Ladd Jr., the then head of production at Twentieth Century Fox. Ladd did not expect the director's 'arty' films to generate any notable profits (he was not looking for another *M*A*S*H*). Altman offered intelligent, adventurous film-making. Any losses incurred by his films (which, given the minimal budgets, would be minor) could be balanced by the studio's big commercial successes. Thus, 1977 saw the release of both *Star Wars* and *Three Women*, the first film in Altman's new Fox deal. He also embarked on his brief stint as a producer of other directors' films (see Appendix).

Altman claims that the idea for *Three Women* came to him in a dream (though what he dreamed was the casting and locations rather than the precise content). He hired Patricia Resnick, a public relations assistant employed at Lion's Gate, to work on a treatment based on the dream and subsequent ideas. Unconcerned with logic or narrative coherence (to the extent of dispensing with a proper screenplay), Altman relied on his instincts in deciding on the film's content. Altman has described hunches as 'the most accurate messages we receive'. This is debatable, to say the least, but in the case of *Three Women*, his hunches paid off.

Filmed on location in Palm Springs, surrounded by vast stretches of desert, *Three Women* is a quiet (even the usual Fox fanfare is absent), haunting dream which intermingles a weird mysticism with a subtle, mocking humour. Like most dreams, there is no satisfactory way of deciphering its exact meaning. Altman calls it a film about 'personality theft', which is true up to a point, after which this idea is transformed into something far more elusive.

The plot has Mildred 'Pinky' Rose (Sissy Spacek) arriving at the Desert Springs Geriatric and Rehabilitation Centre to work as an attendant, looking after the elderly patients. Introverted and childlike (she blows bubbles in her Coca Cola and plays around in a wheelchair), Pinky latches on to co-worker Millie Lammoreaux (Shelley Duvall), an empty-headed woman with sad delusions of sophistication (her idea of a fine wine is 'Tickled Pink') and irresistible sexuality (she hangs around at a nearby hospital and the local bar in the hope of picking up her ideal man). Millie chatters on endlessly about cooking, microwave ovens, recipes, Scrabble, air-conditioning and parking spaces (Duvall wrote most of her own dialogue), unaware that she is either ignored entirely or mocked behind her back. Impressed by Millie's pretensions, the naive Pinky moves in with her (at the Purple Sage Apartments), meekly accepting Millie's condescending attitude and tasteless interior decor (predominantly yellow). Pinky's devotion to Millie ('You're the most perfect person I ever met') is shattered when the latter brings home her drunken landlord, Edgar Hart (Bob Fortier), for a bout of passionless sex. Further upset by Millie's abusive criticism of her ('You don't drink. You don't smoke. You don't do anything you're supposed to'), Pinky throws herself into a swimming pool at the centre of the apartment complex. Taken to hospital, she falls into a coma.

Pinky wakes up with what the doctors term 'temporary amnesia' (she fails to recognize her visiting parents). In fact, she is undergoing a change in personality (and identity) which no pat medical diagnosis can explain. Rejecting her nickname, she insists on being called Mildred. Increasingly

aggressive and selfish, the new Pinky embodies all of Millie's worst traits, exaggerated to a degree which borders on parody. Adorned with make-up 'borrowed' from Millie, she now drinks, smokes and hangs out with the local men (including Edgar), becoming the centre of attention in a way that Millie only dreamed of. She steals Millie's social security number and her car. Pinky is a new, 'improved' version of Millie. Millie, on the other hand, becomes gradually more passive, seemingly helpless as she loses what minimal personality she had.

So far, we have a straightforward (if completely fantastic) case of 'personality theft'. The theme of doubles and twins is present throughout the film. Altman makes much use of reflections in water and glass, duplicating (and fragmenting) various characters. Identical twins work at the clinic, prompting some strange musings from Pinky ('Do you think they know which one they are?'). When Millie fits out Pinky with a bathing suit (much of their time is spent walking patients around the clinic's shallow indoor pool), her dialogue ('You're a little like me, aren't you?') suggests some bond between them. Edgar used to work as Hugh O'Brian's stunt double for the *Wyatt Earp* television show (he still dresses like a cowboy, complete with gunbelt). Most obvious of all, Millie and Pinky share 'Mildred' as a first name.

Had *Three Women* confined itself to this main theme, it would be more coherent but less satisfactory. Apart from anything else, Millie's personality is hardly worth stealing. Moreover, after Pinky's suicide attempt, Millie becomes a nicer, more caring person, staying by Pinky's bedside and tracking down her parents (she even declines a young doctor's offer of breakfast rather than leave Pinky). We share her dismay as Pinky takes on the unattractive traits that she has now lost. The film's change in direction (which, it should be said, some critics regard as a mistake) comes about through the presence of the third woman, Willie Hart (Janice Rule), Edgar's wife and co-owner of the Purple Sage Apartments and the Dodge City bar.

Heavily pregnant, the pallid, near silent Willie spends much of her time painting bizarre murals depicting creatures half human, half reptilian (the film opens with her working on a new mural). Often seen through a watery haze, she has an almost ghostlike presence. One of the murals features three female creatures menaced by a predatory male, a pseudo-mythical representation of the bond between herself, Millie and Pinky and the threat posed to all of them by the lecherous Edgar.

After a vivid nightmare (a blue-tinged sequence featuring transformation, duplication, drowning and murder), Pinky abandons her new identity, reverting to her old self, while Millie takes on a stronger, more maternal personality. Willie's child (a boy) is stillborn (all three women end up with its blood on them, another form of bonding). Edgar is killed in a mysterious shooting 'accident' (he anticipates his demise early on: 'I'd rather face a thousand crazy savages than one woman who's learned how to shoot'). Having freed themselves from the prevailing patriarchal order (so to speak), the three women set up house at Dodge City. Millie and Pinky now have a mother/daughter relationship, while Willie's precise position in this new 'family' remains undefined. As Altman zooms out from the house, the viewer will either be infuriated by this incomprehensible denouement or endlessly intrigued.

Reviewers were sufficiently intrigued for *Three Women* to score as a critical success (though there were a number of detractors). Shelley Duvall's performance earned her a Best Actress award at Cannes. Ladd had got his prestige movie and, as a result, agreed to back Altman's next film, *A Wedding*, on the strength of a treatment running just over ten pages.

Altman's inspiration for *A Wedding* seems to have been threefold. The characters are supposedly based on his own family (though one would hope not). The subject, a big society wedding, offered plenty of scope for satire and black comedy. The scale of the story, incorporating 48 speaking characters, eclipsed even *Nashville*'s epic canvas. All the more pity that Altman and his three co-writers failed to come up with a film worthy of these ambitions.

The two families at the centre of *A Wedding* are the Sloans, who represent inherited wealth and respected tradition, and the Brenners, social climbers with a fortune made from the trucking business. Nettie Sloan (Lillian Gish), the aged head of the family, expires just as her grandson, Dino Corelli (Desi Arnaz Jr.), becomes hitched to Muffin Brenner (Amy Stryker). This is merely the first in a series of misfortunes and revelations (some minor, most catastrophic) which ensue during the course of the day.

Nettie's sudden death aside (fifteen minutes into the film, this rather wastes the talents of Lillian Gish), all is not well in the Sloan family. One daughter, Regina Corelli (Nina Van Pallandt), the groom's mother, is a pathetic heroin addict (the family doctor keeps her supplied). Another is conducting a covert affair with a black member of her mother's staff. The husband of a third has fallen passionately in love with the bride's mother, Tulip Brenner (Carol Burnett). The only remotely sane family member is Luigi Corelli (Vittorio Gassman), father of the groom. Formerly a lowly waiter in an Italian restaurant, Luigi gained acceptance into the Sloan clan only on the condition that he severed all links with his own family. Finally despairing of his snobbish, bigoted and decadent in-laws, Luigi abandons his wife, status and money and flees back to Italy.

The Brenners also have their share of problems, mostly deriving from the antics of Muffin's sister Buffy (Mia Farrow). Silent for most of the film, Buffy speaks only to inform the groom that she is pregnant with his child. Confronted by her irate father, Snooks (Paul Dooley), Dino admits to sleeping with Buffy. He is, however, just one of many (including, towards the end of the film, his visiting uncle). Buffy also parades naked in front of her sister's wedding portrait (a nude, for contrived comic effect), though only a senile Bishop notices. As foolish and selfish as the Sloans, the Brenners exhibit the same sad obsession with maintaining a respectable social façade at all costs. Only Muffin and her epileptic brother seem remotely sympathetic, though their minimal screentime allows no opportunity for character development.

The various calamities reach their climax when the news arrives that the bride and groom have been killed in a car crash. The two families turn on each other, trading deadly insults, only to discover that Muffin and Dino are alive and well (the wrecked car was being driven by Muffin's former boyfriend, accompanied by Dino's former girlfriend). Altman intended this scene to be the most revealing of the entire film, showing all the assembled characters in their true colours, yet the end result is little more than an incoherent shouting match. Nothing new is learned about the various protagonists. Amid the jubilation, Luigi realizes that no-one else cares about the actual victims of the crash and decides to make his exit, first bidding Nettie a respectful farewell.

A *Wedding* contains a number of good moments (the terminally ill

Nettie advising her nurse to quit smoking for health reasons, an ultra-cool security guard responding to the latest disaster by yelling 'Shit. Shit. Shit. Shit . . .') and one has to admire Altman's dexterity in his orchestration of the numerous characters, though few are particularly memorable. As a satire, the film lacks focus (the anti-religious slant is surprisingly under-developed) and much of the humour (such as a blaspheming bishop) is both lazy and obvious. There is an element of deliberate bad taste, with Nettie's corpse reappearing as characters either decide not to let on that she's dead or simply fail to notice, yet even this seems a little tame. Though technically as accomplished as Altman's earlier work, *A Wedding* is a film of missed opportunities, amusing and irritating in about equal measure.

While *A Wedding* was being shot on location just outside Chicago (mostly at the Armour Mansion), Altman put his follow-up film, *Quintet*, into pre-production. An oblique tale of a future society where life revolves around a peculiar boardgame (the 'Quintet' of the title), this particular project met with difficulties from the start. The original writer (Lionel Chetwynd) got no further than the story outline (inspired by another of Altman's dreams) before resigning over money. Patricia Resnick (one of *A*

A Wedding – Luigi Corelli (Vittorio Gassman), Dino Corelli (Desi Arnaz Jr.) and Tulip Brenner (Carol Burnett)

Wedding's co-writers) embarked on the screenplay but felt unhappy with the result and departed to make way for a third writer, Frank Barhydt. Filming on location in wintry Montreal, the cast and crew had to endure great physical discomfort (even in the interior scenes, the actors' breath vaporizes) and a rushed schedule. *A Wedding* had proved to be a critical and financial disappointment and Altman feared that Twentieth Century Fox would withdraw the backing for *Quintet* at the slightest provocation. All he really had in his favour was a star name (Paul Newman once again) and a respected international supporting cast (Fernando Rey, Bibi Andersson, Vittorio Gassman and Brigitte Fossey).

Set in some unspecified future (post nuclear holocaust?) where the world has frozen over and the human race is slowly dying out, *Quintet* follows the adventures of Essex (Newman), a seal hunter, as he returns to the city he abandoned ten years earlier to find his brother. Accompanied by his pregnant wife, Vivia (Brigitte Fossey), Essex discovers a society where all technology has been discarded and the people have reverted to a medieval-style existence. Wild dogs roam the streets, feeding off the corpses of those claimed by the icy weather. The only thing left of any importance is Quintet, a game involving five players stalking each other's pieces around a pentagonal board. Each player must try to 'kill' the others. When only one is left, a sixth player is brought on to challenge the survivor. The élite players are given the chance to take part in the grand tournament, where the game is played for real across the area of the entire city (itself a giant pentagon). Essex's brother turns out to be a tournament player and when he and Vivia are killed by an opponent (via an indiscriminate explosion), Essex decides to join the game. As the various contestants wipe each other out, Essex befriends another player, Ambrosia (Bibi Andersson), only to be forced to kill her in order to win the game (and save his own life). Finally repelled by Quintet's glorification of violent death (the killings, including several throat slashings and a metal skewer through the face, are fairly graphic), Essex leaves the city.

Quintet remains the least popular of Altman's films ('Dismayingly pretentious claptrap' and 'Perhaps the most boring film ever made' are fairly typical assessments) and there is certainly a lot wrong with it. The pace is unusually slow (occasionally grinding to a halt altogether), the plot is difficult to follow, the dialogue tends towards the wilfully obscure, the acting is variable and the relentless sense of nihilism (this is a film with absolutely no sense of humour) can be depressing. Faced with these glaring faults, most viewers will look no further. This is a pity, as there is much in *Quintet* which is actually quite impressive.

Opening (and finishing) with distant figures in a frozen landscape, *Quintet* establishes its sombre mood in a pre-credits sequence as Essex and

Quintet – Essex (Paul Newman) contemplates the enigmas of *Quintet*, a no-holds-barred game of death

Vivia struggle through the snow towards the city (in reality an abandoned exhibition centre). On the soundtrack we have howling winds and a haunting harp score (the film's main musical motif). Dressed in white (seal fur?), Essex seems a part of the natural landscape. Along with Vivia, whose baby will be the first born in a long time, Essex represents mankind's determination to survive. Vivia's murder means the end of any real hope for a future. In a surprisingly touching scene, Essex carries Vivia's body out of the city (where it would be devoured by the scavenger packs) and places her in a river whose current bears her away. Essex will eventually follow his wife back into the natural wilderness (a gesture which can be read as either romantic or utterly futile).

The community within the city is depicted in convincing detail. As various figures huddle around fires, purchase the vital supplies of wood or play

Quintet, there is a sense of a daily routine in progress. Even the corpse-eating dogs seem accepted as a necessary part of this moribund society. The tournament players include Saint Christopher (Vittorio Gassman), a self-styled mystic who views the entire universe as a pentagon with nothing but darkness at its centre. Life is one long game of chance with survival as the only prize (McGilligan calls *Quintet* a 'sci-fi *California Split*'). Saint Christopher's religious devotion to Quintet (he is the champion player) is contrasted with Essex's weary contempt for the whole murderous ritual. The final confrontation between the two men ends in anti-climax. Pursuing Essex across the snowy wastes, Saint Christopher falls down an ice bank and breaks his neck (which surely counts as disqualification).

Ambrosia, while less fanatical than Saint Christopher, is as unwilling to abandon the game. Thus her tentative relationship with Essex (they spend a chaste night together) is only a brief interlude. Disinterested in the past (and holding no hope for the future), Ambrosia accuses Essex of trying to find meaning where there is none (the audience may well agree by this point). Death is always arbitrary, of significance only because it gives life an extra sense of thrill. Living only for the moment, Ambrosia cannot replace Vivia and Essex does not hesitate to kill her, completing the last 'move' of

A Perfect Couple – Alex (Paul Dooley) and Sheila (Marta Heflin)

the game. He then departs, ignoring the demands of Grigor (Fernando Rey), the ubiquitous Quintet judge, that he stay to play again. Essex has always killed to live. He has no place among people who live only to kill.

Quintet met with a dismal reception, placing further strain on Altman's relationship with Twentieth Century Fox. Under pressure, he wisely opted to make his next film a little more accessible. *A Perfect Couple* is a surprisingly (and enjoyably) straightforward romance concerning two 'lonely-hearts' who meet via a video dating agency (then a relatively new phenomenon). Alex Theodopoulos (Paul Dooley) is a middle-aged, middle-class Greek eager to escape from the clutches of his repressive family. Sheila Shea (Marta Heflin) is a backing singer with a rock band. Dominated by his tyrannical father, Panos (Titos Vandis), Alex finds a kindred spirit in Sheila, who, like the rest of her band, is kept under the thumb of the overbearing lead singer, Teddy (Ted Neeley, famous for fifteen minutes as *Jesus Christ, Superstar* (1973)). Needless to say, the Theodopoulos clan does not approve of Sheila (being strictly classical music people) and Alex's budding romance appears to be heading for heartbreak. Even when Panos insults Sheila to her face, Alex offers his own apologies rather than stand up to his father's appalling behaviour. Only his invalid sister, Eleousa (Belita Moreno), offers him any encouragement. Her untimely demise provides Alex with the necessary impetus to break away from his empty existence and seek love and happiness with Sheila.

The script, written by Altman and Allan Nicholls (after acting in *Nashville*, Nicholls became a regular Altman collaborator for a number of years), may be a little uneven and the Theodopoulos family somewhat stereotyped (and not particularly Greek), but these are minor drawbacks. Paul Dooley and Marta Heflin ensure that Alex and Sheila come across as a likeable if unexpected couple, their relationship developing from a mutual need for companionship into a genuine romance. The rock 'n' roll background, including several concert sequences, is well drawn and provides the opportunity for some wild camerawork (courtesy of Edmond L. Koons, whose work on *A Perfect Couple* recalls the fluid style perfected by Altman in his collaborations with Vilmos Zsigmond). The film also makes the point that the supposedly free and easy world of sex and drugs and rock 'n' roll can be as oppressive and stifling as any other 'family' grouping. *A Perfect Couple* might lack the ambition of other Altman films, but following on from the detached, overly-cerebral *Quintet*, it has an engaging vitality. Alas, Twentieth Century Fox did not know what to do with it and the film was barely reviewed, let alone released.

An even worse fate befell the political satire *Health*, Altman's last film for Fox. Shot very quickly on location at the Don Cesar Hotel in Florida (as with *Quintet*, Altman feared that any delays could cost him his financing),

Health was finished in time for a release in the summer of 1980, when the ongoing Presidential election campaign would have given it a particular relevance. Unimpressed by either the film or Altman's apt timing, Fox's distribution division branded *Health* uncommercial and shelved it for two years.

A scattershot satire in much the same style as *A Wedding*, the film centres on a health food convention held by the H.E.A.L.T.H. organization (Happiness, Energy And Longevity Through Health). The major event of the meeting is the election for H.E.A.L.T.H.'s new president. Esther Brill (Lauren Bacall) is the popular candidate, an 83-year-old virgin (each orgasm shortens a life by 28 days) with a line in punchy, if meaningless slogans such as 'Raise your hands for purity.' Her main rival is Isabella Garnell (Glenda Jackson), an honest, anti-'showbiz politics' candidate who rejects materialist values and espouses human ideals. A third, independent candidate, Dr Gil Gainey (Paul Dooley, who also co-wrote the script with Frank Barhydt and Altman), does little more than fall into swimming pools and peddle his 'Vital-Sea' pills, guaranteed to ensure good health. As the campaigns swing into action, a gullible White House advisor, Gloria Burbank (Carol Burnett), attempts to lend covert support to Isabella Garnell, while her womanizing ex-husband, Harry Wolff (James Garner), works as Esther Brill's campaign manager. After various escapades involving a political dirty tricks specialist, Bobby Hammer (Henry Gibson), and the mysterious 'Colonel Cody' (Donald Moffat), Esther Brill wins the election by a landslide. All this takes place under the bemused eye of television chat show host Dick Cavett (as himself), who ends up wishing he had covered the forthcoming hypnotists' convention instead.

With the parallels between the H.E.A.L.T.H. election and the US Presidency contest explicitly spelt out (several times), *Health* scores a number of easy points (Esther Brill could well be a close cousin of Ronald Reagan) without ever finding the edge or sureness of touch that distinguishes *Nashville*. Bobby Hammer attempts to discredit Isabella Garnell by convincing Gloria Burbank that her preferred candidate is a transsexual (donning drag, he pretends to be a former navy colleague who underwent the same operation). Gloria is then harassed by Colonel Cody, who claims to be both the real boss of H.E.A.L.T.H. and the 'top man' in the country. Yet these devious goings-on hardly seem necessary, as Gloria has no influence over popular opinion (thus the revelation that Cody is in fact Lester Brill, Esther's mad brother, counts for little). Furthermore, Esther's overwhelming victory indicates that Isabella never stood a chance. Harry Wolff argues that no-one could understand the latter, but much the same could be said for Esther Brill. Her victory seems more the result of her showbusiness-style campaign (shades of *Nashville*) than her opponent's unintelligible manifesto or any 'dirty tricks'.

Health – Isabella Garnell (Glenda Jackson)

Most of the main characters exhibit the expected Altman eccentricities. Esther has a habit of falling into a trance-like sleep, with her right arm sticking in the air (a Nazi salute?). Isabella smokes huge cigars and dictates endlessly into a miniature tape recorder. Gloria becomes sexually aroused when scared, enabling Harry to renew their close relationship on a couple of occasions. All this comes across as a little forced, recalling the random weirdness of *Brewster McCloud* rather than the carefully etched idiosyncrasies of *The Long Goodbye* or *Three Women*. The jokes vary from the predictable (everyone eats junk food or drinks or smokes in secret) to the successfully offbeat (all the security men are dressed as vegetables). Perhaps *Health*'s strongest asset is its gaudy carnival atmosphere, complete with hucksters and suckers (a handy metaphor for most aspects of American society).

As his once-promising deal with Twentieth Century Fox reached its rather sad conclusion (*Health* would eventually play to American audiences in only two cinemas nationwide), Altman found his career in a bad way. Always something of a fringe figure in Hollywood, with a reputation for publicly attacking any studio, star, union or critic he felt aggrieved by, he was now regarded as a talent in decline. Altman had never been a profit-oriented film-maker and his lack of critical success since *Three Women* left the major studios little reason to employ him. In fairness, a portion of the blame for this drastic slump in his fortunes must fall on Altman. His last few films had been decidedly uneven, betraying a certain overconfidence in some cases (*A Wedding*) and an ill-advised haste in others (*Health*). The fact that there was still enough talent in evidence to lift these films far above the standard mainstream output counted for little with critics eager to demolish Altman's reputation. Few even bothered to look at *A Perfect Couple*, in many ways the director's best film since *Three Women*. Fox seem to have given up on Altman after *A Wedding* and Alan Ladd Jr.'s departure from the studio following a management reshuffle left his work at the mercy of disinterested marketing men. Amid all this indifference, however, there was one producer left with faith in Altman's talent. Shortly after completing *Health* he was hired by Robert Evans to direct *Popeye*, a multi-million-dollar musical for all the family.

Created by comic-strip artist Elzie Crisler Segar, Popeye the Sailor Man first appeared in 1929 as a supporting character in Segar's *Thimble Theater* series, which followed the adventures of the Oyl family (Olive, Castor, Cole and Nana). An immediate success, he soon became the hero of the strip, winning the affections of Olive Oyl. In 1933, Popeye made the transition to the big screen in the first of many animated shorts produced by Max Fleischer (father of *Bodyguard* director Richard Fleischer). Distributed by

Paramount, the cartoons proved highly popular and the Fleischer studio continued to turn them out until 1950. The highlight of these films was usually a prolonged battle between Popeye and his arch-enemy Bluto, a black-bearded, black-hearted ogre with evil designs on Olive Oyl. Having been thoroughly pounded, pummelled and stomped on by Bluto, Popeye would lay his hands on a can of spinach (the source of his great strength), swallow the contents whole, flex his muscles and beat Bluto senseless. Television gave the cartoons continued exposure, with audiences so enthusiastic that several new (if inferior) series were made. Not surprisingly, Paramount opted to retain their rights to the character.

Robert Evans' interest in turning Popeye into a live-action musical dated back to 1977, when he was outbid for the rights to the hit Broadway musical *Annie* (also based on a popular comic strip). Formerly a production executive at Paramount (overseeing hits such as *Barefoot in the Park* (1967), *Rosemary's Baby* (1968) and *The Godfather* (1972)), Evans had continued his association with the studio as an independent producer, enjoying critical acclaim and commercial success with *Chinatown* (1974) and *Marathon Man* (1976). Paramount already owned Popeye, so Evans hired satirical cartoonist Jules Feiffer (also the screenwriter for *Carnal Knowledge* (1971) and *Little Murders* (1971)) to produce a script based on Segar's characters. Dustin Hoffman agreed to play the title role, with Lily Tomlin co-starring as Olive Oyl. Hal Ashby (whose *Harold and Maude* (1971) gave *Brewster McCloud* star Bud Cort his best role) signed on as *Popeye*'s director.

Had all proceeded smoothly, Altman would not have got a look in on *Popeye* (just as he would not have been given *M*A*S*H* had any one of fifteen other directors recognized its potential). Fortunately for him, unfortunately for Ashby, Tomlin and Hoffman, the latter argued with Feiffer over the screenplay. Evans backed his writer rather than his star (despite the fact that they had just made *Marathon Man* together) and Hoffman walked out on the project. The resulting delay obliged Ashby and Tomlin to follow suit in order to meet pre-existing work commitments. Undeterred, Evans decided that *Popeye* did not need a star name. His final choice, Robin Williams, was inspired. A successful stand-up comedian, Williams had achieved small-screen celebrity as the star of *Mork and Mindy* (his co-star, Pam Dawber, appears briefly in *A Wedding*). Paramount went along with Evans' decision to cast Williams, even though he was making his film debut in a far from easy role. They were less enthusiastic about Altman (the success of *Nashville* now being ancient history). Evans had an ability to match the right talent with the right vehicle, however (Francis Coppola's pre-*Godfather* career hardly made him the most obvious choice for the film), and the studio went along with his wishes.

Evans had no particular interest in resurrecting Altman's career (both Mike Nichols and Arthur Penn were considered before him). He simply recognized that the director's offbeat talent could be ideal for the equally offbeat style of *Popeye*. Once Altman was in place, Evans left him in charge while he supervised another film (the John Travolta vehicle *Urban Cowboy* (1980)) being shot simultaneously. Assembling many of his past collaborators, Altman selected the island of Malta as his location and commenced filming early in 1980. *Popeye* offered him his first real chance of a major commercial hit since *Nashville*. He had his largest-ever budget (estimates vary between $20 and $30 million) and the guarantee of a wide release (territories were to be split between Paramount and co-producer Disney). Success would give him the kind of status he hadn't enjoyed since *M*A*S*H*. Failure could finish him as a mainstream film-maker.

Popeye is an unqualified success, a rare example of a family film (Altman's first and only excursion into this field) which provides adults with as much to enjoy as children. Its main achievement is to reproduce the style and spirit of the original cartoons, remaining faithful to both Segar and Fleischer, while carefully developing the characters and situations into feature length material. Perhaps its most unusual accomplishment is to have actors play cartoon figures as real people, involving the audience in their misfortunes and triumphs. The look of the film is extraordinary (rather like the community of *McCabe and Mrs Miller* seen while under the influence of some mind-altering substance), with equal credit going to Altman, cameraman Giuseppe Rotunno, production designer Wolf Kroeger and costume designer Scott Bushnell.

Jules Feiffer's script (reworked in collaboration with Altman) opens with Popeye arriving at the port of Sweethaven in search of his father, Poopdeck Pappy (Ray Walston), who abandoned him thirty years earlier. Though apparently a contented place ('Sweet Sweethaven', as the opening song goes), there is much unhappiness. The town is run by the mysterious, unseen Commodore, whose brutal second-in-command, Captain Bluto (Paul Smith), keeps everyone in line, while the nosy Taxman (Donald Moffat) takes all their money (there is even an 'embarrassing the Taxman tax'). Met with a less than friendly welcome, Popeye finds lodgings with the Oyls. Olive Oyl (Shelley Duvall) is reluctantly engaged to Bluto, though she makes no pretence of being flattered. When she flees from her engagement party, Bluto demolishes the Oyl's house (while singing 'I'm mean').

At first preoccupied with the quest for his lost father, Popeye is gradually drawn into the world of Sweethaven. He falls in love with Olive (their romance is beautifully played) and finds an abandoned baby, Swee'pea (Wesley Ivan Hurt, Altman's grandson). This new-found family is completed when Popeye discovers that the Commodore is none other than his father. Tired of being a dictator ('It's not easy being mean'), Poopdeck Pappy joins forces with Popeye, who after a protracted battle defeats Bluto with the aid of a can of spinach.

All the main characters resemble their cartoon originals to an almost unnerving degree (Altman told Shelley Duvall that she was born to play Olive Oyl). Robin Williams is Popeye in the flesh, with permanent squint, jutting jaw and awesome forearm muscles. Those who complained about Altman's trademark use of overlapping dialogue and sound effects in the film conveniently ignored the fact that he was only following on from the Fleischer cartoons. Popeye's mumbling, muttering, often semi-coherent pattern of speech is one of his major characteristics. When the early cartoons were made, the characters' mouths were not animated to synchronize with the scripted dialogue, leaving the voice-actors plenty of scope for improvisation.

The songs used in *Popeye* are amusing and, on occasion, surprisingly witty ('I'm no physicist but I know what matters'). Altman chose pop composer Harry Nilsson to supply the music and lyrics (Leonard Cohen was also considered) and was rewarded with a score that contributes to both the entertainment and the characters without disrupting either the mood or pace of the overall film. One of Popeye's solos, 'I Yam What I Yam' articulates the main theme. Oppressed by Bluto, the people of Sweethaven behave as they are told to, not as they wish. Even the hamburger-guzzling Wimpy (Paul Dooley), one of the town's few disreputable figures, meekly complies with Bluto's orders. Popeye is always true to his nature and his vanquishing of Bluto (who literally turns yellow) gives others the freedom to be themselves. The film concludes with a rousing rendition of Sammy Lerner's 'I'm Popeye the Sailor Man'.

The violence in *Popeye*, while in the over-the-top, wholly unreal style of the cartoons (Popeye is flattened several times, only to bounce back like rubber), is carefully thought out. Popeye does not look for trouble. Like Altman's Marlowe, he endures the crude taunts of others rather than resort to violence. When Bluto's gang of toughs goad him, mocking his appearance and accent, he grows angry only when they insult his long-lost father (who, unlike the similarly absent Terry Lennox, proves himself worthy of such loyalty). Having trounced the toughs, Popeye subsequently takes on the giant-sized boxing champion Oxblood Oxheart (Peter Bray), a particularly mean octopus and, of course, Bluto. In every case he fights either to defend another person or teach a bully a lesson.

The shooting of *Popeye* had its share of mishaps and 'creative differences'. Altman clashed with both Feiffer (who eventually came round to the director's way of thinking) and Nilsson (who left the production a little earlier than expected). Bad weather caused delays in filming, as did problems with some of the special effects (Williams' first set of artificial muscles tended to split under strain). These were hardly disastrous setbacks (and certainly not unique to this one production) yet rumours of chaos on the set and escalating costs filtered back to Hollywood, giving Altman the kind of publicity he could well do without. Many had written *Popeye* off before the film even opened.

Released in late 1980, *Popeye* never managed to lose its 'failure' stigma. Reviewers either reacted with a shrug of incomprehension or damned it with faint praise. Dismayed at this reception, Disney re-edited the film before releasing it in Britain. Several scenes were shortened, losing a lot of the more eccentric dialogue and some of the slapstick violence. A duet between Popeye and Olive as they watch over sleeping Swee'pea was deleted. Further songs were taken off the soundtrack, though the accompanying action (such as Bluto's rampage through the Oyl residence) remained in abbreviated form. This kind of tampering only reinforced the idea that Altman had produced a flop. In fact, *Popeye* achieved a respectable, if unspectacular, worldwide gross of $60 million, recovering its costs at the very least (which is more than can be said for the second Paramount/ Disney co-production, *Dragonslayer* (1981), a resounding box-office failure). This, as McGilligan says, made the film Altman's most popular since *M*A*S*H*. Breaking even was not enough, however. As far as the big studios were concerned, *Popeye* only served to confirm Altman's status as a has-been.

Popeye – Olive (Shelley Duvall) and Popeye (Robin Williams), a perfect couple

7

Dimes, Fools and Therapy

Now widely regarded as unemployable in Hollywood, Altman was obliged to scale down his film-making operations. In 1981 he reluctantly sold his production company, Lion's Gate, which had also been operating (with modest success) as a state-of-the-art post-production facility for hire. Determined to keep his career on the rails, Altman picked up the rights to a play, *Lone Star*, a comedy involving a Vietnam veteran, and approached the newly merged MGM/UA for a deal. With Sigourney Weaver and Powers Boothe lined up for the leads, the film seemed a possibility. MGM/UA dropped the project, unhappy with Altman's bad publicity following the *Popeye* fiasco. United Artists had only recently suffered a near fatal financial disaster (hence the merger) with Michael Cimino's *Heaven's Gate* (1980) and the new management felt little inclination to take chances. Altman also attempted to secure backing for *Easter Egg Hunt*, a tale of sexual repression (from a script by Gillian Freeman) intended for filming in Montreal. Similar to *That Cold Day in the Park* in both subject and location, the project did not attract the necessary finance. (Hardly surprising. Aside from Altman's difficulties, Freeman's screenwriting career had never really gained momentum; her few post *Cold Day* film credits, such as the risible sex-change melodrama *I Want What I Want* (1971), attracted little attention).

With no film work on the horizon, Altman opted to switch his attentions to the theatre, directing a new play on Broadway, *Come Back to the Five and Dime, Jimmy Dean, Jimmy Dean*. Written by Ed Graczyk, this small-town story of empty dreams and painful revelations provided an effective, if patchy, vehicle for its cast, which included Altman veterans Sandy Dennis, Karen Black and Marta Heflin along with pop star Cher, then a relative newcomer to acting. Critics failed to appreciate either Altman's direction or the fine performances and the play received dismissive reviews, closing after a short run. Nevertheless, it spurred Altman (who'd financed the production with his own money) to return to film-making, if only to produce a permanent record of a play he felt had been unfairly derided. Retaining the original theatre cast, he made a deal with production executive Peter Newman to film *Come Back to the Five and Dime, Jimmy Dean, Jimmy Dean* for screening on cable television. Altman's only previous venture into filmed theatre, *Buffalo Bill and the Indians*, had proved a failure, albeit an interesting one. This time around, he had a property he believed in and more than an expedient interest in seeing it succeed. Shooting on Super 16mm film (a long way from 35mm Panavision) within the confines of a single set and a $850,000 budget, Altman came up with an emotionally powerful drama let down only by the flaws of the original play.

Set entirely within the cramped space of a Woolworth's Five and Dime, the drama unfolds during the course of one day, September 30th 1975 (the twentieth anniversary of Dean's death), as the former Disciples of James Dean gather for a reunion in their home town of McCarthy, Texas. Dean's last film, *Giant* (1956), was shot only a short distance from the town (a crumbling exterior set still stands) and the store is filled with star memorabilia. Two of the disciples have remained in McCarthy (a spurious political reference). Mona (Sandy Dennis) works as a clerk at the Five and Dime, run by the devoutly religious Juanita (Sudie Bond). Sissy (Cher) is a waitress whose main aim in life is to hold on to her reputation as the most desirable woman in town. As they wait for the other disciples to arrive, we are repeatedly taken back twenty years to discover why these two are still hanging on to a world they should have left behind many years before.

The flashbacks to 1955 introduce Mona and Sissy's best friend Joe (Mark Patton), who lost his job at the Five and Dime when Juanita's husband, Sidney, discovered he was gay. Unwilling to suppress his homosexuality, Joe even put on drag (for a joke), fooling the local macho man, Lester T. Callaghan, into believing he was a girl. After being badly beaten up by Callaghan, Joe left town for good. In an act of extreme disloyalty, Sissy ended up marrying Callaghan, the prize catch among the local men.

Mona's attachment to McCarthy is a little more unusual. Employed as an extra in *Giant*, she claims to have been James Dean's lover, bearing his child as a consequence. The boy, Jimmy Dean, was put on public display at the store, a nine day wonder for the curious. Twenty years on, her moment of fame long past, Mona is still religiously devoted to Dean. Her son (who never appears) is mentally retarded, still the child who once pulled in crowds.

The reunion attracts three visitors. Edna Louise (Marta Heflin), pregnant with her seventh child, works in a beauty parlour. Stella Mae (Kathy Bates) is an uningratiating loudmouth whose wealth fails to compensate for

Come Back to the Five and Dime, Jimmy Dean, Jimmy Dean — Mona (Sandy Dennis), Sissy (Cher) and Joanne (Karen Black)

ner taste in ridiculous 'cowgirl' outfits. The third arrival turns out to be Joe, who, following a sex change operation, is now Joanne (Karen Black). Of the assembled women, only Joanne has come to terms with the past and herself, confident in her identity. Her presence forces the others to confront the illusions which have stunted their lives.

First into the confessional is Sissy, whose much-flouted sexuality (her breasts being the main attraction) masks a private misery. After developing breast cancer, she underwent a double mastectomy. Desperate to keep her figure, the only reason why men give her a second glance, Sissy took to wearing rubber 'falsies'. Unimpressed, her husband abandoned her (she pretends that he is working abroad) to look for a 'real' woman. On his travels he ran into the recently transformed Joanne and tried to pick her up (a rather contrived touch of irony). Slightly lower down in the trauma stakes, Juanita is forced to accept that her late husband was a drunken womanizer, a moral hypocrite no better than Lester T. Callaghan.

This catalogue of revelations goes into overdrive when it comes to Mona's turn. Initially one of the more sympathetic characters, refusing to subscribe to the prejudices and small-mindedness of the other townsfolk (hence her friendship with Joe), she gradually falls apart before our eyes as her treasured memories suffer the same fate. For starters, no-one ever seriously believed that James Dean really was the father of her child. The town welcomed the publicity (Sidney got himself elected mayor on the strength of it) and let Mona keep her delusions. Nor is Jimmy Dean the simple-minded 'child' she claims. Anxious to hold on to the most important part of her James Dean fantasy, she refuses to let her son grow up. Finally (and perhaps one 'shock' too many), Joe is revealed as the real father of the boy, conceived when he and Mona spent a night together while waiting to be cast for the crowd scenes in *Giant*.

Like the more surreal *Images, Come Back to the Five and Dime, Jimmy Dean, Jimmy Dean* is in part an attempt to explore the way women are forced to suppress their emotions and personalities in order to be accepted by the male-dominated society around them. As with the earlier film, the issue is blurred by the insistence that the characters are also victims of their own illusions and foolishness. (It does not help that they are shown the way to 'liberation' by a man, transsexual or not.) There is also the familiar Altman concern with celebrity, though here it is more a case of celebrity by proxy as Mona attempts to retain just a little of the James Dean mystique left over from her 'association' with the star. Subtract James Dean from Mona's life and there is virtually nothing left. She even threw away the chance of a college education (blaming her supposed ill-health) rather than leave the scene of her moment of glory.

Scripted by Graczyck with no input from Altman, the film suffers mainly from some weak dialogue (theatrical in the worst sense) and poorly developed supporting characters. Stella Mae is the least successful of these, leaving Kathy Bates (later to win an Academy Award for her performance in *Misery* (1990)) with little to do. An attempt to give Stella a measure of depth (she is infertile and secretly longs for a child) seems little more than an afterthought. Much the same can be said about Sissy's claim that Jimmy Dean (who drives off in Joanne's car) is not retarded at all. It is difficult to respond to a character who exists only through the accounts of other characters. We can only take Mona's (or Sissy's) word.

Working with Canadian cinematographer Pierre Mignot for the first time (Mignot would serve as Altman's regular cameraman for six films in a row), Altman turned his failed stageplay into a properly cinematic experience, transcending the limitations of the 16mm format (his preference for slightly off-focus visuals renders the inferior picture definition relatively unimportant) through expert direction (mercifully free of the uncomfortable close-ups and static long shots that plague much filmed theatre) and precision editing. The film's time zones are ingeniously linked via a mirror which runs the length of the wall behind the store counter. The mirror becomes a window into 1955, enabling the characters to gaze into the past.

Newman was sufficiently impressed with *Come Back to the Five and Dime, Jimmy Dean, Jimmy Dean* to agree to a small-scale theatrical release for the film (Altman's intention all along). Reviews proved largely positive (*Monthly Film Bulletin* reviewer Richard Combs went as far as to call the film 'Altman's masterpiece'), with particular praise going to the lead performances. Cher continued her acting career, quickly working her way up to star status (in films such as *Silkwood* (1983), *Mask* (1985), *Moonstruck* (1987), *The Witches of Eastwick* (1987) and *Mermaids* (1990)), while Altman found himself with both a successful film and a modest profit.

It is tempting to look on Altman's move into filmed theatre as a deliberate step, with the director no longer able to tolerate the inane demands of the commercial mainstream. While he enjoyed a fair amount of acclaim for *Come Back to the Five and Dime, Jimmy Dean, Jimmy Dean*, it is unlikely that Altman intended to make a new career for himself in independent 'prestige' cinema. Finance remained as difficult to come by as ever. His next film, *Streamers*, had existed as an unrealized project for a number of years before reaching the screen in 1983.

David Rabe's play, a claustrophobic study of four young army recruits waiting to be sent to Vietnam, had made its stage debut back in 1976 (directed by Mike Nichols). Altman secured the film rights, intending to embark on a cinema version straight away, but couldn't raise the backing. Seven years on, he met with a similar level of indifference and when *Streamers* went into production at Last Colinas Studios (near Dallas), the budget came out of Altman's own pocket. Rabe provided the screenplay (Altman would take a co-writing credit on only one of his filmed plays, *Beyond Therapy*) while *Popeye* designer Wolf Kroeger came up with the single set, a drab army barracks. Altman's son Steven, who'd worked on a number of his father's films in a variety of capacities, took his first credit as a fully-fledged art director.

Streamers (the title refers to parachutes that fail to open) is an uncomfortable but often powerful drama. The Vietnam conflict provides the setting for an examination (somewhat inconclusive) of the tensions existing within American society during the sixties, with the emphasis on racism and homophobia. The opening credits play over a group of backlit soldiers carrying out a tightly choreographed drill routine (reminiscent of a musical production number without the music), throwing their rifles about like drum majorettes' batons. This is a faceless squad of trained automata. The film shows us the 'real' people behind this façade.

Streamers – Carlyle (Michael Wright)

The barracks that comprise the whole world of *Streamers* (the occasional glimpses outside reveal very little) are home to three raw recruits, Richie (Mitchell Lichtenstein, son of Pop artist Roy Lichtenstein), Billy (Matthew Modine) and Roger (David Alan Grier). Richie is a spoiled rich kid (hence his name, presumably) who covers his loneliness by adopting a casual attitude, flaunting his supposed wit and intelligence in a somewhat effeminate manner. Billy, though priding himself on his streetwise manner, has an educated middle-class background. Roger, the only black soldier in the barracks, is easygoing and well adjusted to the tedious routine of army life. Billy is pro-Vietnam (he compares the Vietcong to Hitler and the Nazis), but has not yet accepted the realities of war (the idea of people killing 'don't seem possible'), while Richie claims not to care. His 'queer' behaviour antagonizes Billy, though he and Roger accept Richie on the grounds that he only acts that way to provoke them.

The recruits share their quarters with two veterans, Rooney (Guy Boyd) and Cokes (George Dzundza), who make occasional drunken appearances, playing mean practical jokes and shouting a lot. The camaraderie between the men is uneasy at best, with Rooney hurling random abuse ('shitsacks') at regular intervals. That said, the older men do not single Roger out for racist taunts, treating him just the same as Billy and Richie. Cokes is a decorated war hero haunted by the acts of violence which earned him his medals. Now diagnosed as suffering from leukaemia, he won't get the chance to kill (or be killed) for his country again.

This fragile sense of community is broken by the arrival of Carlyle (Michael Wright), another black soldier. His 'outsider' status is underlined by an introductory shot placing him outside the barracks looking in. Gaunt and aggressive, Carlyle sees himself as being at the bottom of the social heap ('I got nothing'). He latches on to Roger, alternating between overtures of friendship and ill-concealed malice. In a moment that recalls Wade's attack on Tommy Brown in *Nashville*, he accuses Roger of being a traitor to his 'brothers', having an easy time with a 'couple of dick-head white boys'. Not content with creating friction between Roger and Billy (the latter regards the newcomer as dangerous), Carlyle pushes Richie to admit that he's gay (a 'punk'). Richie resists until he realizes that he has a chance for sex with Carlyle, who propositions him after a night on the town. Once Richie has made his homosexuality overt, Billy and Roger can no longer fool themselves that he's just a 'little effeminate'. Billy, for all his claims that 'queers can be okay', is repelled by the thought of gay sex and hurls racist abuse at Carlyle ('You fucking sambo'). Carlyle stabs Billy, inflicting a fatal wound, and deals out the same fate to Rooney when the latter returns from a drinking binge. Carlyle is arrested, leaving Richie to weep (over the dead?) while Roger turns away from the 'faggot' with sad contempt.

The determinedly downbeat subject matter is matched by the sombre visuals. The colour scheme is similar to that of *M*A*S*H* (uniform greens, dark wood browns) but without the bursts of colour. There is no vitality here, only the deep red of spilled blood (a botched suicide attempt early on in the film anticipates the two stabbings towards the end). Altman again avoids the static quality associated with filmed theatre, maintaining a brisk pace through editing and observing the regime of barrack life in close detail. His only lapse is a certain heavy-handedness in the closing stages, as when he cuts to a black military policeman each time the man's commanding officer says 'nigger'.

Streamers proved another *succès d'estime*, earning praise and Golden Lion Best Acting Awards at the 1982 Venice Film Festival for all six principal members of the cast. The film is regarded by some as Altman's most successful eighties work, though there is a case for arguing that the characters represent a slightly too obvious cross section of American society, while Carlyle's self-pity and near psychotic violence alienate him from any audience sympathy.

Unlikely as it may seem, Altman's subsequent project, *O.C. and Stiggs*, began life as a highly commercial property. Peter Newman, a close friend of the director after *Jimmy Dean*, had commissioned a script based on a National Lampoon story (*The Ugly, Monstrous, Mindroasting Summer of O.C. and Stiggs*, written by Tod Carroll and Ted Mann) about two anarchic teenagers creating havoc in a small Southern town. *National Lampoon's Animal House* (1978) had been a smash hit for Universal and youth pictures, usually involving crude humour spiced with a little female nudity, could still generate big box-office receipts. *Porky's* (1982), a deeply crass Canadian production, had made a fortune in American cinemas. The major studios wanted to get in on the act and several bid for the rights to *O.C. and Stiggs*.

It is doubtful that Altman ever felt any great enthusiasm for the script, essentially a running battle between the wild teenagers and the uptight, ultra-patriotic Schwab family. What he did appreciate was a good opportunity to re-establish himself as a commercial director. Newman agreed to make Altman a part of any deal and the film was sold to MGM/UA as a surefire cross between *M*A*S*H* and *Nashville*. Still a little uncertain about Altman, the MGM/UA executives obtained his assurance that the script would be filmed as written (to the letter) before handing over the $7 million budget. As soon as he was safely on location in Phoenix, Arizona, Altman embarked on a large-scale rewrite. Despite his best efforts (or because of them) *O.C. and Stiggs* turned out to be a fairly dismal film, unredeemed by its few bright moments.

The flimsy plot involves Oliver Cromwell Ogilvy (Daniel H. Jenkins) and his best friend Mark Stiggs (Neill Barry) making life miserable for local insurance salesman Randall Schwab (Paul Dooley) as revenge for his treatment of O.C.'s grandfather, Gramps (Ray Walston). Schwab cancelled the latter's life insurance, condemning him to spend the rest of his days in a retirement home. While pursuing their vendetta, the boys encounter such wacky characters as a crazed Vietnam veteran (Dennis Hopper), a campy dress designer who employs slave labour, a sad alcoholic who eventually dies (they bury him on a golf course) and a couple of gay teachers who make an easy target for blackmail. Schwab's family consists of an alcoholic wife (her attempts to hide her liquor inside binoculars and plastic ice cream cones make for a rather feeble running joke), a dimwit son and a perpetually whining daughter. The rambling, episodic narrative is padded out by a lengthy musical interlude (courtesy of King Sunny Adé and his African Beats) before grinding to a halt with a pathetic finale involving the Schwab's nuclear shelter, a helicopter and some fireworks.

Burdened by two distinctly unlikeable leading characters (who specialize in 'smartass' repartee and cruel practical jokes), *O.C. and Stiggs* is quite

O.C. and Stiggs – Stiggs (Neill Barry) struts his stuff, accompanied by his ever loyal 'sluts'. The film's casual misogyny is merely one of many glaring defects

astonishingly unfunny, lacking any sense of wit or invention. After the MGM Lion shouts 'O.C. and Stiggs' instead of his usual growl, it's downhill all the way. Altman attempts to liven up the proceedings with a few irrelevant film references in the form of mini *homages* to *A Wedding*, *Brewster McCloud* (bird shit), *Nashville* (Hal Philip Walker appears on the Schwab's television), *The Wizard of Oz* and *Apocalypse Now*. The performances lack much sense of direction, with only Ray Walston managing to extract any real humour from his character. A former policeman, Gramps likes to reminisce about his gorier cases in great detail. This black humour may not be in the best of taste but it's all the film has to offer.

During the filming of *O.C. and Stiggs* (which took place under uncomfortably high summer temperatures), Altman fell out with the management at MGM/UA, eventually breaking off communication with them. Relations were not improved during post-production, when it became painfully obvious that the film didn't work. Former colleague Lou Lombardo attempted to re-edit Altman's footage into a releasable product but resigned after disagreements with the director. Stuck with Altman's cut of *O.C. and Stiggs*, MGM/UA tried the film out on a preview audience. The response proved so hostile that the studio shelved the film until 1987, when it appeared very briefly in order to clear the rights for a video release.

Altman quickly turned his attentions back to the theatre, taking a particular interest in a one-man show about former President Richard Nixon. *Secret Honor*, by Donald Freed and Arnold M. Stone, follows the drunken rantings of the fallen leader over the course of one night at the Oval Office as he attempts to explain his life, his presidency and the Watergate scandal to an unseen judge. After seeing the play during its initial run at the Los Angeles Actors Theatre, Altman arranged its transfer to an off-Broadway theatre in New York before embarking on a film version. Working with minimal resources, he shot *Secret Honor* at the University of Michigan with 16mm equipment. The original stage director, Robert Harders, worked with star Philip Baker Hall on his performance, enabling Altman to concentrate his attentions on the technical side of the production.

Of all the director's filmed plays, *Secret Honor* comes closest to being a relatively straight record of a work conceived for another medium. As with *Jimmy Dean* and *Streamers*, there is only the one set, though here Altman adds an extra dimension of space through the use of four security monitors lined up on a table in Nixon's office. For those not put off by the format (no opportunity for character interaction), the film is an effective piece of drama, sustained through its compact running time (85 minutes) by Baker Hall's energetic performance and Altman's probing camera.

Subtitling itself as 'a fictional meditation' and 'an attempt to understand',

Secret Honor – Richard Nixon (Philip Baker Hall) and friend

Secret Honor begins with Nixon arriving at the Oval Office (we see him approaching via the television monitors), determined to reveal the truth behind Watergate. In a jokey reference to the Watergate tapes, he attempts to make a recording of his 'confessions', first forgetting to insert a cassette into the machine, then failing to press the record button (he gets it right on the fourth attempt). At first sidetracked by fond memories of his family (whom he compares to the Kennedy clan), especially his Quaker mother, Nixon goes over his career, recalling the humiliations (J. Edgar Hoover turned him down for the FBI) and the betrayals. As he gives vent to his rage, portraits of former Presidents (with the emphasis on such 'greats' as George Washington and Abraham Lincoln) stare down impassively. There is a long 'hate list', starting with the Founding Fathers of the United States ('a bunch of snotty English shits'), the despicable Kennedys, Henry Kissinger ('a whoremaster'), the media and liberals. Everyone is an 'unindicted co-conspirator'. Controlled by the mysterious Committee of One Hundred (a group of faceless businessmen), Nixon was forced into a series of immoral deals, prolonging the Vietnam War in exchange for millions of dollars and forming a secret anti-Soviet pact with China. Unable to tolerate the evils perpetrated in his name, he deliberately leaked the Watergate tapes in order to lose his popularity (after winning the presidency in 1968, Nixon was re-elected in 1972 in a landslide victory) and destroy any chance of a Republican win in 1976. His public shame masks a secret honour. Nixon contemplates taking his own life (a gun lies on the desk), but decides not to give his enemies the satisfaction of seeing him self-destruct ('Fuck 'em'),

Altman's direction stresses Nixon's sense of imprisonment. He is a victim of both the presidency (the window of the office is lit to resemble prison bars) and the media. The camera repeatedly zooms in on the television monitors, showing a man trapped by his public image. Even as Nixon shouts his climactic defiance, Altman returns to the monitor screens with frenetic camera movements, reducing his protest to four lifeless freeze frames, while the familiar election cry of 'four more years' dominates the soundtrack. Altman may not have taken any part in the creation of the stage original, but *Secret Honor* is in many ways his final word on politics and celebrity. Baker Hall portrays Nixon as a hollow, pathetic man who seeks redemption through the destruction of his public façade. This Nixon at least deserves the viewer's pity. The only weakness in the performance is a tendency to lapse into a predictable series of mannerisms (a stream of

Fool for Love – May (Kim Basinger)

invective will become increasingly incoherent, finally disintegrating into mumbled obscenities) for dramatic impact.

Having got through 1983 with an unreleasable flop and an acclaimed, if non-lucrative, art movie, Altman once again found himself seeking both projects and finance. Sam Shepard, a respected writer and actor, had offered him the film rights to his play *Fool for Love*, the love in question being incestuous. Altman hestitated over accepting the property (though he'd touched on similar ground in *That Cold Day in the Park*) until Cannon Films presented him with a production deal he couldn't refuse. Cannon, founded by executive producers Menahem Golan and Yoram Globus, specialized in violent action movies such as *Death Wish II* (1982) and *Delta Force* (1985). Anxious to upgrade their company's image, Golan and Globus were on the lookout for more prestigious vehicles and decided that *Fool for Love* was ideal for their requirements (Cannon's other up-market productions included John Cassavetes' *Love Streams* (1984), Andrei Konchalovsky's *Duet for One* (1986) and Franco Zeffirelli's *Otello* (1986)). Not wishing to skimp on prestige, they supplied Altman with a $6 million budget and he headed off to Santa Fe to shoot the film with Sam Shepard and Kim Basinger in the roles of the tempestuous lovers.

Set in and around the Mojave Desert Motel (this was the first of Altman's filmed plays to employ exterior locations), *Fool for Love* tells the unlikely story of May (Basinger) and Eddie (Shepard), people as desolate as the landscape they move in. May works at the motel, which also includes a diner and a gas station (all exterior sets purpose-built for the film). Her only company is an old man (Harry Dean Stanton) who lives in a caravan nearby. Eddie, a cowboy stuntman, drives into the motel complex, seeking to reclaim May as his lover. When she refuses to come out to him, he smashes through the door of her bungalow. May accuses Eddie of abandoning her for another woman, the Countess, but this is only a minute part of their love/hate relationship (May follows a passionate embrace with a knee in the groin). Having met and fallen in love as teenagers, they subsequently discovered that they shared the same father, a man who led two separate lives with their respective mothers. May's mother broke down when she lost her bigamous husband for good. Eddie's mother shot herself. They have been tormented by their incest ever since, each looking for love elsewhere but unable to forget the other ('We'll always be connected'). Their father, the old man with the caravan, merely lingers in the background, apparently oblivious to the damage he has caused.

The most interesting aspect of *Fool for Love* is the way it plays with past and present (no magic mirrors here). A small girl playing in a sand pit outside the motel turns out to be May as a child, an all too solid ghost/memory embraced by the adult May (like several other Altman heroines, she finds comfort only in her past) as an innocent reminder of her life before Eddie. When the film flashes back to her teenage romance with her half-brother, the accompanying narration (supplied by Eddie and May in turn) seems a little out of step with what we are shown. The past (it seems) can never quite be recaptured, however far-reaching its effect on the present.

Altman brings a fair amount of style to *Fool for Love*, framing his characters either through or against windows to underline the sense of entrapment and isolation, without quite managing to overcome the flawed screenplay. Shepard employs too many 'profound' lines, such as 'it was the same love. It just got split in two', or 'I was gone, but I wasn't disconnected', which (on film at least) seem merely risible. Despite solid performances (Basinger in particular) the characters are never quite believable and the introduction of the Countess, with her limousine and her .357 Magnum pistol, tips the film into grim farce. During the puzzling denouement, the Countess sets the motel complex ablaze and drives off with Eddie (on horseback) in pursuit. May packs a suitcase and heads off down the highway, leaving her father to play his harmonica as the motel burns. Though undeniably striking at times, *Fool for Love* is overlong and overwrought.

Released to mixed reviews, *Fool for Love* did little for either Cannon's image or Altman's career. Many felt that the director should have stuck to his single-set approach rather than opening the play out into a more naturalistic setting (which is certainly at odds with the deeply melodramatic content). Cannon's (over)generous investment made little impact on the film (the relatively high budget does not show onscreen) or the box office. Altman would not shoot another film in the United States for seven years. In 1985, he moved to France, setting up a production base in Paris (where much of the post-production work on *Fool for Love* was completed). There were no immediate offers of film work, so he concentrated his attentions on television, directing a production of *The Laundromat* (1985), a play by Marsha Norman, starring Carol Burnett. This was followed by two Harold Pinter plays, *The Dumb Waiter* and *The Room* (both 1987), filmed in Montreal for the ABC network. Altman intended to make use of his new location (*The Laundromat*, as McGilligan points out, could have been shot anywhere) with a whodunnit set during the bi-annual Paris *Pret a Porter* fashion show, but the idea got no further than a script (though *Pret a Porter* did later go into production, financed by Miramax Films, with Lauren Bacall, Tim Robbins and Kim Basinger cast in the leading roles).

Altman continued to work on film projects, including *Across the River and Into the Trees*, an adaptation of an Ernest Hemingway story intended for Roy Scheider and Julie Christie. These quickly joined his long list of might-have-beens. In 1986, he received an unexpected offer to direct *Heat*

(1987), an action vehicle for fading star Burt Reynolds. The script, by William Goldman (who'd done rather better with the likes of *All the President's Men* (1976) and *Marathon Man*), was strictly to formula, an uninspired mixture of slick violence and 'buddy' humour. It presented Altman with another chance to improve his credentials as a bankable director and he seriously considered accepted the job before giving in to his better judgement (memories of *O.C. and Stiggs* may have influenced his decision). His reservations turned out to be justified. After a traumatic production (involving a change in director) *Heat* proved a commercial failure.

A rather more serous loss to Altman was his missed chance to make a sequel to *Nashville*. Jerry Weintraub, an executive producer on the original film, had interested Paramount in a follow-up using the original cast, writer Joan Tewkesbury and Altman. Intended for release in 1987, the project stumbled at the script stage. Tewkesbury disliked the proposed storyline (reputedly even more downbeat than the original), obliging Altman to find another writer. The resulting screenplay did not meet Weintraub's requirements and, amid the arguments over rewrites, the *Nashville* sequel stalled.

Back in France, Altman embarked on another filmed play, Christopher Durang's *Beyond Therapy*, financed by New World Pictures. This New York tale of frustrated romance, eccentric psychiatrists and bisexuality cannot have been the most obvious choice for location filming in Paris (Altman appears to have given up on the pretence, ending the film with a shot of the Eiffel Tower). The incongruous background detail is in fact the least of its problems. Despite a good cast, including Jeff Goldblum, Julie Hagerty (best known for her role in *Airplane!* (1980)), Glenda Jackson and Tom Conti, *Beyond Therapy* is a disaster.

Even in outline, the film offers few opportunities for humour or insight. Prudence (Hagerty), a nervous young woman in search of a 'real' man, arrives at a restaurant to meet up with her blind date, who turns out to be Bruce (Goldblum), an amiable bisexual bored with his male lover. After a less than successful meeting (they end up throwing water in each other's faces), they both visit their therapists. Prudence confers with Stuart (Conti), who advises her to go to bed with him, while Bruce attempts to explain his problems to Charlotte (Jackson), who rarely listens to a word her patients say. In the meantime, Bruce's lover, Bob (Christopher Guest, one of the talents behind the celebrated spoof 'rockumentary' *This is Spinal Tap* (1984)) learns through his overbearing mother of Bruce's treachery. After a tedious series of events (alternating between the restaurant, Bruce and Bob's apartment and the psychiatrists' offices), Prudence (no longer quite so prudish) and Bruce decide they were made for each other, while Bob takes up with a young waiter, who also happens to be Charlotte's son.

Beyond Therapy – Stuart (Tom Conti) and Charlotte (Glenda Jackson) look on as Bruce (Jeff Goldblum) and Prudence (Julie Hagerty) celebrate their new-found love. In the background, Bob (Christopher Guest) socializes with a young friend. An awkwardly posed publicity shot for a painfully unfunny comedy

The script (co-written by Durang and Altman) is poorly contructed, with weak dialogue ('Sometimes you're so insensitive it just makes me wanna puke') and an unsuccessfully 'zany' sense of humour. Stranded with unplayable roles, the actors give awkward performances (the French actors filling the supporting roles are painfully miscast), often verging on the inept. Bruce's offbeat behaviour (he compliments Prudence on her breasts after they have known each other for around thirty seconds) is peculiar rather than amusing. Prudence's seemingly intractable dislike of gay men (even crying is unmanly) vanishes a little conveniently. Bob is a stereotyped homosexual, mincing and pouting, and his relationship with Bruce is never made convincing. As the psychiatrists, Glenda Jackson and Tom Conti struggle to extract any sense of character from their roles. Jackson gives an understated, non-committal performance, while Conti, miscast as a New Yorker posing as an Austrian (or possibly an Italian), seems deeply ill at ease.

Beyond Therapy also fails as a piece of film-making. The problems of shooting on location without an adequate budget result in a dull visual surface, with dim lighting and unimaginative design. Most of the familiar Altman devices (reflected images, slow zooms, overlapping dialogue) seem here either half-hearted or misused. The film has little sense of reality to it, but resolutely refuses to take off into the fantastic or the surreal. *O.C. and Stiggs* is merely a bad film. *Beyond Therapy* is a bad Robert Altman film. Their appearance in the same year (1987) marked the nadir of his career.

8

Vincent and Theo
and Griffin

After the embarrassment of *Beyond Therapy*, Altman once again found his career in limbo. Though the film had been received as a disappointment rather than a disaster (some reviewers even liked it), its failure brought his filmed theatre phase to a halt. His last venture into cinema during the eighties amounted to little more than the directors' equivalent of a cameo role. In 1988 British producer Don Boyd hired Altman to work on the ambitious opera vehicle *Aria* (1988), along with nine other directors. The idea behind this feature-length work was for each film-maker to produce a visual interpretation of a chosen aria, a classical music version of a pop video. Altman settled on three pieces from Jean Philippe Rameau's *Les Boréades*, accompanying the music with a group of eighteenth-century lunatics (inspired, perhaps, by William Hogarth's contemporary illustrations for *The Rake's Progress*) supposedly watching a performance of the then brand new opera. While hardly a major piece of work, his segment is at least lively and interesting to look at. Taken as a whole, *Aria* is a misconceived venture, with many of its contributors (among them Bruce Beresford, Jean-Luc Godard, Derek Jarman, Franc Roddam, Nicholas Roeg and Ken Russell) resorting to banal, pretentious or ridiculous imagery (including a laughable updating of Richard Wagner's *Tristan and Isolde*).

1988 also saw Altman back in television, directing *The Caine Mutiny Court Martial* and *Tanner '88*. The former, scripted by Herman Wouk from his novel (also the basis for the 1954 film *The Caine Mutiny*, starring Humphrey Bogart), proved a solid piece of drama, with impressive performances from Brad Davis and Michael Murphy. Murphy also starred in *Tanner '88*, a satirical series following the adventures of a fictitious political candidate interacting with the real candidates involved in the ongoing election campaign. Working with cartoonist/writer Gary Trudeau, Altman produced a consistently entertaining show that scored with viewers and critics alike, picking up an Emmy (American television's top award) for Best Director. Further awards followed from French and British television (Best Foreign Series in both cases). *Tanner '88* may not have brought the Hollywood executives knocking on Altman's door, but it gave his reputation a much-needed boost at a time when his film career was experiencing a prolonged pause.

This pause (which continued well into 1989) finally came to an end when producer Ludi Boeken contacted Altman with an invitation to direct *Vincent and Theo*. Altman liked the script (by British writer Julian Mitchell), with its emphasis on Van Gogh the flawed, disturbed man as opposed to Van Gogh the Great Artist, and accepted the assignment. The theme of the neglected artist 'punished' for living before his time may have struck more than a few chords. Determined to create as authentic a portrayal as possible, he did his own in-depth research into the life of the nineteenth-century Dutch Post-Impressionist. Financed largely by British and French money, *Vincent and Theo* was shot in Holland and France over an eleven-week period, using the original locations wherever possible. The supporting cast consisted entirely of Dutch and French actors, the only concession to the international market being the casting of two British actors in the leading roles, with Tim Roth as Vincent and Paul Rhys as Theo. Altman brought several of his old collaborators with him to the project, including costume designer Scott Bushnell, cameraman Jean Lepine (Pierre Mignot's regular assistant and director of photography on *Tanner '88*) and art director Steven Altman.

Van Gogh had already been given the Hollywood biopic treatment, with Vincente Minnelli's *Lust for Life* (1956), a ponderous, overly reverential Cinemascope epic. *Lust for Life* covers much the same ground as *Vincent and Theo* (often scene for scene), though the earlier film sketches in more of Van Gogh's dismal family background and his failed attempt to become an evangelist preacher. As the tortured artist, Kirk Douglas' performance, while praiseworthy in intent, is often more earnest than anguished, as if the actor felt overawed by his subject. His Van Gogh finally seems a pathetic, irresponsible man, undeserving of any sympathy. Theo (James Donald), here very much a supporting character, is a down-to-earth figure, his troubled private life unexplored. The verbose script contains some intrusive Americanisms (not helped by the odd mixture of accents) and throws in irrelevant spectacle (a number of crowd scenes) when it should be trying to build an intimate portrait. By detailing the lives of both brothers, Mitchell and Altman (who 'developed' the script during filming) avoid the mistakes of *Lust for Life*, revealing both Vincent's misery and his genius through his relationship with Theo.

Vincent and Theo opens in the recent past, as one of Vincent's famous

'Sunflowers' paintings goes up for action. As the price rises by at least a million pounds with each bid, we are taken back to the nineteenth century and the inauspicious start of the artist's brief career. Having just forsaken the Church, the impoverished Vincent now seeks God in art, almost hysterical in his desire to become a painter. The neatly attired Theo, a junior art dealer in their uncles' Paris firm, looks on in dismay. The film then chronicles Vincent's attempts to seek guidance from the respected artists (he is quickly disillusioned), set up house with a prostitute (who models for him) and her two children, study art as a 'proper' pupil and establish an artists' commune with Paul Gauguin. Theo continues to disapprove, but supplies his brother with money (he makes nothing from his paintings) for materials and food. He grows to recognize Vincent's talents while others remain indifferent. Theo's own life, though more conventional, has its share of frustrations and disappointments. Dealing in the business of art, he is obliged to sell work he dislikes to ignorant clients interested only in 'fashionable' pictures. His love life is equally troubled, with one relationship abruptly terminated after he contracts syphilis. Marriage to a friend's sister proves unfulfilling, despite the birth of a son, with the initial romance soon displaced by tiresome arguments over money.

As portrayed by Tim Roth, Vincent is a difficult man, obsessive, ungrateful and demanding. Art is his religion; anything else is a secondary consideration. Unconcerned with the opinions of polite society, he lives with a prostitute, Sien (Jip Wijngaarden), attempting to act as a husband and father while developing his talent (this short-lived 'family' is contrasted with one of Theo's flings as a swinging single). Eager to work from life as opposed to artifice, Vincent draws Sien with fervour as she squats on a chamber pot. She objects, wanting to be pictured as a model, not herself. Later on at art college, he waits till the paid model falls asleep before drawing her, capturing the person rather than the professional. On arriving at the college, Vincent wanders amid a sea of art students, all dressed in the traditional white smock and black beret, a uniform that he will never wear. Throughout, Altman places great emphasis on the sheer physical labour involved in painting (in an interview he argued that 'the value of art is not in its existence, but in its doing'). Frequently covered in paint, Vincent must spend hours cleaning brushes, preparing canvases and mixing colours before he can embark on the act of creation.

Vincent's obsesssion begins its inexorable slide into insanity during his time in Provence with Gauguin (Wladimir Yordanoff), a painter with a style wildly at odds with his own. Known as an exotic, sensual artist, Gauguin is fussy, organized and methodical in both his work and his life. Vincent mocks Gauguin's anti-bourgeois pretensions (he will buy only the cheapest paints) and heads off into a sunflower field. As the nodding flowers look on

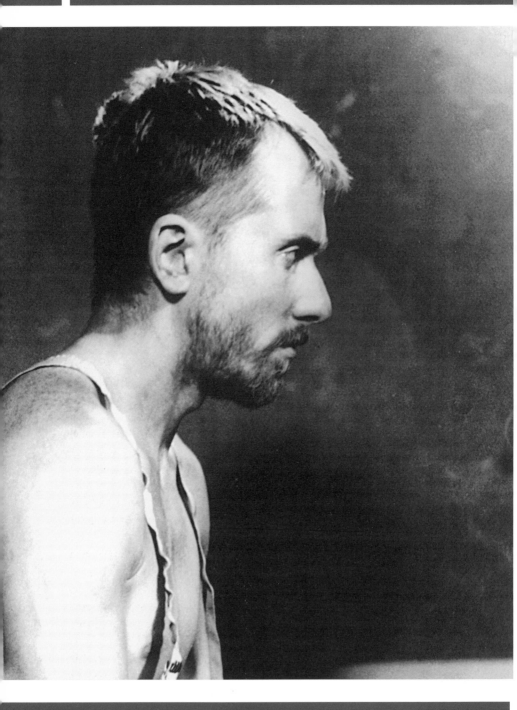

Vincent and Theo – Vincent Van Gogh (Tim Roth)

like a silent audience (Altman films the field as a living crowd), Vincent attempts to paint them, finally giving up in a rage (he destroys the canvas). He cuts a handful of the sunflowers and takes them indoors for a still life. Vincent's differences with Gauguin finally boil to the surface in an argument over cooking, the latter supplanting the former's slapdash approach with his precision. When Gauguin decides to leave for Paris, Vincent threatens him with a knife. A violent storm reflects his growing inner turmoil (hardly an original device, but effective nevertheless). Vincent screams into a broken mirror, his sanity as fragmented as his reflection. His famous act of self-mutilation follows, as he slices off his left earlobe (a moment as excruciating as *The Long Goodbye* Coke bottle in the face), licking the blood off his knife. A brief sojourn in an asylum produces an outward calmness but the sense of inevitable self-destruction persists.

Placed in the care of Dr Gachet (Jean Pierre Cassel), a friend of Theo's, Vincent attempts to turn himself into a tame artist, only to meet with hypocrisy and lies. Gachet professes to be an art lover (the world is merely a bad painting which should have been destroyed), but keeps his collection in a bank vault. He encourages painting as a form of therapy, failing to realize that Vincent's madness and creativity are inextricably intertwined. Having overheard Gachet describe him as incurably insane, Vincent walks out into a cornfield one sunny day with his easel and canvas and shoots himself. Altman frames the suicide attempt in long shot, distancing the viewer as Vincent collapses in an almost comical fashion (some startled blackbirds take flight). He then gets up (clutching his bleeding side) and staggers back home to die soon after with Theo at his bedside. The scene of his suicide reappears as a painting (complete with birds in flight). Even Vincent's death takes second place to his art. In spite of all the pain, rejection and breakdown, there is a sense that he knows the true worth of his work. As the final bid for the auctioned 'Sunflowers' is announced (£22.5 million), Vincent is seen grinning in close-up.

Theo's relationship with Vincent, as brother, friend, patron (his house is full of his brother's pictures) and father-figure, carries a fierce sense of devotion. His 'madness' may be less flamboyant than Vincent's, but it is no less intense. Determined to succeed as a businessman (though his colleagues suspect him of favouring art over commerce), he puts up with his uncles' patronizing behaviour until they give him his own gallery to run (once out of their sight, he leaps for joy). Like Vincent, Theo has to be his own man, and will not be told by his brother how to run his business or market Vincent's pictures. Each must respect the other's territory. The bond between the brothers is expressed in a bizarre scene where both respond to being abandoned by their respective partners by sitting in front of a mirror and smearing their faces, Theo with rouge and Vincent with paint. Theo's marriage to Jo Bonger (Johanna Ter Steege), after a touchingly awkward courtship, fails to provide the stability he needs. Jo, while good-natured, cannot comprehend the depth of his feelings for Vincent, eventually responding to their relationship with angry frustration. After Vincent's suicide, Theo gradually loses his own grip on life, following his brother through the asylum to the grave in the space of a year (Altman reduces Theo to a mere shadow on a wall as he weeps beside Vincent's deathbed). The film's final image is their gravestones, side by side, marked with only their names and dates.

Altman's direction of *Vincent and Theo* follows a relatively straightforward style, with only limited use of his customary slow zooms, overlapping dialogue and ironic humour. Jean Lepine's photography is low-key (mostly brownish hues) but attractive, capturing both the squalor and the art integral to Vincent's way of life. The music alternates between a jarring, discordant electric guitar and synthesizer score (echoing Vincent's disturbed state of mind) and a gentler, melancholy piano and strings theme. Though well over two hours long (the version released to television runs even longer), the film's pace rarely flags (the Gauguin episode drags a little, a case of history interfering with narrative flow) and the compelling leading performances hold the attention throughout.

Released to rave reviews, *Vincent and Theo* revived Altman's career, enjoying a level of acclaim he'd not experienced since his peak in the mid-seventies. During the film's production, both *McCabe and Mrs Miller* and *The Long Goodbye* were re-released (in London and Paris respectively) with considerable success. Altman intended to follow *Vincent and Theo* with another biopic, this one depicting the life and times of the nineteenth-century Italian composer Rossini. After a brief period of preproduction discussions in Rome in late 1990, the project stalled. Altman decided the time was right to try his luck back in the United States with a new project, *LA Short Cuts* (later known as *Short Cuts*), a multi-character, multi-story drama combining loose adaptations of short stories by Raymond Carver with original material. The trip proved worthwhile, despite the initial lack of interest in the *Short Cuts* idea (Paramount agreed to finance the screenplay, written by Altman and Frank Barhydt, only to reject the finished script). Altman was offered another project, *The Player*, a Hollywood-on-Hollywood satire produced by an independent company, Avenue Entertainment. Scripted by Michael Tolkin from his novel (Tolkin also acted as one of the film's three producers), *The Player* is an amusing parody of the industry's worst excesses, its scathing examination tempered by an undeniable affection (despite his clashes with the big studios, Altman wisely avoids any trace of bitterness). This is Hollywood poking fun at itself, rather than a detached outsider looking in, but no less effective for it.

Sticking fairly closely to Tolkin's book, *The Player* follows the fortunes of Griffin Mill (Tim Robbins, who replaced original choice Chevy Chase), a big shot story executive with one of the major companies. The studio is in a state of unease, with rumours of an impending takeover casting a shadow over the daily routine of phone calls, meetings and deals. Griffin is unsettled by the appointment of a new executive, Larry Levy (Peter Gallagher), widely touted as his replacement-in-waiting. Everywhere he goes, Larry keeps appearing on the scene. A more immediate threat arrives in the form of a series of mysterious postcards. At first merely abusive ('I hate your guts asshole'), the cards soon take on a more disturbing tone ('In the name of all writers, I'm going to kill you'). Checking back through his appointment records, Griffin decides that the man behind the threats is David Kahane (Vincent D'Onofrio), an unproduced screenwriter. After spying on the writer's house and his live-in girlfriend, June (Greta Scacchi), Griffin tracks Kahane down at an arthouse cinema showing Vittorio de Sica's *Bicycle Thieves* (1948). Griffin attempts to pacify the writer with an offer of a film deal. Kahane taunts him, suggesting that Larry Levy is now the man to make deals with. A fight breaks out, during which Griffin accidentally kills the writer.

A new message ('Surprise!') arrives the next day. Griffin has killed an innocent man. He attends the writer's funeral, becoming friendly with June. Police Detective Susan Avery (Whoopi Goldberg) arrives at the studio to question Griffin about his meeting with Kahane. Under suspicion of murder, Griffin attempts to hold on to his career. Offered a terrible script about capital punishment (*Habeas Corpus*), he persuades Larry Levy to put it into production, intending to secure his position by riding in to rescue the film when it turns out to be a disaster. Meanwhile, his relationship with June develops into a serious romance and the police summon him to take part in an identification parade. The supposed witness picks out the wrong man (one of the investigating officers) and Griffin walks free.

A year later, Griffin is the new head of the studio. After a disastrous preview, *Habeas Corpus* is now a great success with its new, upbeat ending (courtesy of Griffin). On his way home to June, now his wife, Griffin receives a call from the postcard writer offering him a script about a film producer who kills a screenwriter he wrongly suspects of sending him threats. If the money's right, a happy ending is guaranteed.

The Player is perhaps the ultimate movie about movies. The opening lines, 'Quiet on the set. Action!', put the entire film in cinematic inverted commas. Altman opens with an incredibly elaborate crane shot, several minutes in duration, as the camera prowls around the studio lot, eavesdropping on various characters. This jokey homage to the opening shot of Orson Welles' *Touch of Evil* (1958), a film recalled with nostalgia by a studio security guard ('today it's all cut, cut, cut'), sets the overall tone. The good old days of great movies are long past. Today's studio bosses are more concerned with running tours for potential overseas investors. Projects can only be sold as rehashes of tried and tested ingredients: *The Graduate Part 2* (proposed by Buck Henry, co-writer of the original film), *Out of Africa* meets *Pretty Woman*, *Ghost* meets *The Manchurian Candidate*. A pitch for a 'political' film quickly becomes 'politely politically radical but funny'. When Larry Levy suggests that writers could easily be removed from the 'artistic process', he isn't joking. Griffin can make all the speeches he likes about the need for greatness in films ('Movies are art, now more than ever'), safe in the knowledge that no-one will take him seriously.

Moving among the likes of Rod Steiger, Peter Falk, Angelica Huston, Jack Lemmon and Burt Reynolds (a large number of actors, hired for token fees, make split-second appearances as themselves, a device first used by Altman in *Nashville*), Griffin shouts greetings, shakes hands and promises meetings, never meaning a word he says. After Kahane's death, he finds his life taking on all the ingredients of an overheated crime melodrama, the kind of film his studio would love. His clumsy attempts to make the killing look like a robbery gone wrong come straight out of a bad script. There are multiple references to Hitchcock thrillers and *film noir*. We see posters for *They Made Me a Criminal* (1939) and *Highly Dangerous* (1950). An advert for the 1951 remake of Fritz Lang's *M* (1931) promises 'the worst crime of all'. Griffin begins to experience all the classic symptoms: guilt, suffering, paranoia (the postcard writer could be anyone), with retribution surely just around the corner. Taken to the police station for questioning, Griffin finds events progressing from melodrama to surrealism. Detective Avery twirls a tampon in the air while asking increasingly direct questions about his relationship with June ('Did you fuck her?'). The assembled police officers greet Griffin's protests with mocking laughter. Altman finishes the scene with a close-up of Griffin's sweating face, as he loses all control. The viewer shares his sense of disorientation, sympathizing with Griffin's bizarre plight. He may be manipulative and amoral (and guilty of manslaughter at the very least) but this is the way the movie game is played.

The *Habeas Corpus* subplot ties in fairly well with the main storyline. A pretentious English director attempts to sell the film to Griffin on the strength of its 'important theme' and 'real people'. The ending must be downbeat (a woman is wrongly executed for the murder of her husband) because 'that's how life is'. There will be no star names. The director's streetwise agent quietly plugs Bruce Willis and Julia Roberts for the leads. Though faced with the possibility of ending up in the gas chamber himself, Griffin sees the film only as a chance to outmanoeuvre Larry Levy. Needless to say, the film is turned into a star vehicle for Willis and Roberts with a new nick-of-time rescue climax (Bruce shoots out the glass of the gas chamber just as Julia begins to choke on the fumes). Griffin gets his own happy ending by accident rather than design, but it's still in the best Hollywood fairytale tradition. Now king of his movie castle (until the next flop or takeover bid, at any rate) he drives home to his idyllic house, the Stars and Stripes fluttering on the porch. June, several months pregnant, stands ready to greet him. As the end titles roll, violins soar on the soundtrack.

Where *The Player* comes slightly unstuck is in its portrayal of David Kahane and June. Kahane is an angry young writer caricature, complete with round-framed glasses, stubble, attitude and a severe haircut. A fellow writer orating at his funeral wears exactly the same uniform. Kahane seems to have little affection for June ('the ice queen'), comparing her with Griffin, a bitter enemy. There seems little doubt that he was not a very talented writer. The script he offered Griffin concerns the unexciting adventures of an American student spending a year in Japan (based on Kahane's own experience). An excerpt from his last project read out at the funeral is a stream of tired clichés. Kahane's dislike of happy endings (would he have

The Player – June (Greta Scacchi)

approved of his own?) was not his only problem. Commercial or highbrow, mediocrity is everywhere in this world.

June, a similarly untalented artist who refuses to sell her work (in Tolkin's book she is more convincingly drawn as a commercial designer employed by a bank), fails to register even as a caricature. There seems to be no reason why she and Kahane were together. She claims not to have mixed with his circle of friends or even rated him as a competent writer. (Is Altman trying to make a point about the emptiness of relationships in a soulless world?) She doesn't like watching films or reading, seeking emotional rather than intellectual stimulation (obviously she has never seen one of Griffin's movies). Burdened with silly dialogue, the character remains poorly developed. The scenes between June and Griffin are often contrived and unconvincing. When the latter attempts to explain what happened to Kahane (during a sex scene consisting of faces in extreme close-up), she doesn't want to know. Thus any sense of doubt over Griffin's sincerity towards June becomes irrelevant.

The film's circular ending, with Griffin arranging a deal to make the film the audience has just seen, was added by Altman to the original script (which, like the book, concludes with Griffin secure in his position as head of the studio). As with the opening cry of 'Action!' and the *Habeas Corpus* film-within-a-film, this serves to emphasize *The Player* as a cinematic joke at Hollywood's (and its own) expense. It also recalls the self-referential conclusions of *M*A*S*H* and (to a lesser extent) *Brewster McCloud*. There is a slightly incestuous feel to the film, with many Altman collaborators (Frank Barhydt, Rene Auberjonois, Karen Black, Cher, Paul Dooley, Jeff Goldblum, Elliott Gould, Sally Kellerman, Patricia Resnick, Joan Tewkesbury, to name but a few) appearing either in brief character roles or as themselves. Thankfully, it avoids being either excessively self-indulgent or merely one long in-joke. Altman has been playing the Hollywood game (on and off) for over forty-five years, usually to his own version of the rules, and *The Player* is as much a celebration of film-making as a mock-lament over the idiocies of the film business. The film community decided that it was in on the joke, the critics handing out ecstatic reviews and the industry rewarding Altman with an Academy Award nomination as Best Director, his first since *Nashville*. While *The Player* might not reach the heights of the earlier film, it stands as a striking affirmation of Altman's enduring talent and determination.

9

Short Cuts to Pret a Porter

Armed with the critical raves, awards and respectable (if not quite smash hit) box office receipts garnered by *The Player*, Altman could finally put his long cherished *Short Cuts* script into production. Opting not to take the project back to Paramount (the arguments over the screenplay, not helped by a change in management at the studio, had never been resolved), Altman remained with Avenue Entertainment (now called Avenue Pictures). Originally wary of the *Short Cuts* project, executive producer Cary Brokaw was now prepared to take a chance (on the strength of both *The Player* and his good working relationship with Altman), and a deal was made at the 1992 Cannes Film Festival. As the film which would cement the director's American 'comeback' (Altman liked to protest that he'd never been away), *Short Cuts* could scarcely be more risky. Altman had chosen to take on the work of Raymond Carver, one of modern American literature's most respected figures and (with the approval of Carver's widow, poet Tess Gallagher) transform it into an epic, three hour ride through the casual corruption, violence, lust and banality of a society devoid of any sense of morality or responsibility. This is very much a return to *Nashville* country (making comparisons with the earlier film inevitable), Carver's short stories providing the basis for 22 main characters (arranged into eight family groups), each with their own thread of storyline. Despite the disappointments of *A Wedding* and *Health*, Altman wanted another shot at equalling (or even surpassing) his earlier masterpiece.

As usual, Altman assembled a team of veteran collaborators, notably Scott Bushnell, Allan Nicholls, Frank Barhydt, Steven Altman and Geraldine Peroni (editor on *Vincent and Theo* and *The Player*). The cast included old hands Lily Tomlin, Robert Doqui (both of whom appeared in *Nashville*) and Matthew Modine, *Player* actors (and walk-ons) Tim Robbins, Fred Ward, Peter Gallagher, Lyle Lovett, Andie MacDowell, Jack

Lemmon, Buck Henry and Annie Ross, plus Altman newcomers Bruce Davison (the rat enthusiast in *Willard* 1971), Julianne Moore, Tom Waits, Ann Archer, Jennifer Jason Leigh and Madeleine Stowe (among others). The ten week shoot commenced in August 1992 (on location in and around suburban Los Angeles), with Altman filming each 'family' story segment in turn (roughly a family a week) beginning with the characters played by Tomlin and Waits. The production was recorded for a 'making of…/behind the scenes' film documentary, *Luck, Trust and Ketchup: Robert Altman in Carver Country* (1993), produced, directed and photographed by Mike Kaplan and John Dorrie.

On the face of it, Altman's choice of Raymond Carver (who died of lung cancer in 1988, two years before Altman came upon his work) for cinematic adaptation/re-interpretation seems a little unlikely. Dealing mainly with blue collar, lower middle class losers, with dead-end jobs and dismal home lives, Carver's stories (set in the small towns and drab suburbs of the Pacific Northwest) are written in a precise, spare prose style, detached and dryly amusing. An unsurpassed observer of human foibles, Carver has some sympathy for even the most selfish and petty minded of his characters, most of whom are too wrapped up in the tacit hypocrisies and absurdities of their day-to-day existences to notice much of those around them. Altman has cited Carver's ability to capture 'the wonderful idiosyncrasies of human behaviour… amid the randomness of life's experiences' as his inspiration for *Short Cuts*, though this summation is equally applicable to much of his own work (Carver was a declared fan of *Nashville*). While this feeling of common ground appears entirely valid, the stumbling block of how to transpose the minimalist source material onto celluloid (many of Carver's stories are less than ten pages long) led Altman to a radical solution both wildly ambitious and ultimately misguided.

To place Altman's Carver adaptation in some kind of context, it should be noted that film compendiums based on esteemed literary originals have an honourable, if intermittent, track record. The British distributor Rank released three films taken from short stories by W. Somerset Maugham, *Quartet* (1948), *Trio* (1950) and *Encore* (1951), with considerable success (Maugham co-wrote the screenplay for *Trio*, and made personal appearances in all three in the form of an introduction). Partly to cash in on this success, Twentieth Century Fox produced *O.Henry's Full House* (1952), introduced by John Steinbeck (O.Henry being dead). Pier Paolo Pasolini drew on the works of Giovanni Boccaccio and Geoffrey Chaucer for his sex and violence and slapstick versions of *The Decameron* (1971) and *The Canterbury Tales* (1972), while Paolo and Vittorio Taviani offered a more restrained treatment of stories by Luigi Pirandello in *Kaos* (1984). On a more populist (and exploitative) level, tales by Edgar Allan Poe and

Nathaniel Hawthorne provided the basis for the horror compendiums *Tales of Terror* (1962) and *Twice Told Tales* (1963). And let us not forget the all-dancing *Tales of Beatrix Potter* (1971). In every case, these films treat the original stories as independent entities, one episode following on from another as a self-contained narrative. Uninterested in producing literal adaptations of the Carver originals, Altman departed from this approach, breaking the stories down into their component characters and incidents to produce what he described as 'Raymond Carver soup', from which a vast *Nashville*-style epic was assembled. Altman justified this drastic reworking on the grounds that (a) he wanted to reproduce the spirit rather than the letter of Raymond Carver, and (b) Carver's body of work is really one big story anyway, a vast series of occurrences. Altman's cavalier attitude to source material had resulted in outstanding work in the past, *The Long Goodbye* being an obvious example. *Short Cuts*, sadly, is at best a flawed 'masterwork'. Despite the best efforts of Altman and Barhydt, nine remixed short stories do not an epic make (the cited poem, *Lemonade*, figures only in terms of its theme: the futility of looking for reasons why in the wake of a tragic event). At its strongest, especially on a stylistic level, the film is the equal of *Nashville*, a dazzling display of technique and imagination. At worst it amounts to no more than an ugly soap opera, a clumsy, vulgar bastardisation of Carver's work.

The eight principal families in *Short Cuts* (and their accompanying stories) are as follows:

Earl Piggot (Tom Waits), a chauffeur with a drinking problem, and Doreen Piggot (Lily Tomlin), a diner waitress leered at by customers and ill-treated by her husband. Doreen is tired of arguing with Earl about his behaviour ('drooling' over her daughter, Honey) but is unable to make a final break from him ('he's all I've got').

Howard Finnigan (Bruce Davison), a television news anchorman, and Ann Finnigan (Andie MacDowell), devoted wife and mother. Their son, Casey (Zane Cassidy) is knocked down by Doreen Piggot's car on the eve of his eighth birthday, the same day Ann orders a special baseball cake for him. Though his injuries at first appear minor, Casey dies in hospital the following day.

Next door to the Finnigans are Tess Trainer (Annie Ross), a bitter and cynical jazz singer based at a rather sleazy club, and her daughter Zoe Trainer (Lori Singer), a sensitive classical cellist with an apparent death wish. Like most of the other characters, these two never really connect with each other. Pushed over the edge by the news of Casey's death (and unable to express her despair to Tess), Zoe kills herself in a carbon monoxide-filled garage.

Claire Kane (Ann Archer), a professional clown and Stuart Kane (Fred Ward), an unemployed salesman and keen amateur fisherman. On a fishing

trip with two friends (they first stop off at the diner to get a good look at Doreen's arse/ass), the men discover the naked body of a young woman floating in the water. They decide to finish the fishing ('prime trout time') before reporting the corpse to the police. Disgusted by Stuart's callous attitude, Claire attends the woman's funeral (the newspapers report her as a rape/ murder victim), yet this gesture seems to bring little sense of consolation.

Ralph Wyman (Matthew Modine), a hospital doctor in charge of Casey Finnigan's case, and Marian Wyman (Julianne Moore), a pretentious artist specialising in nudes (her dialogue, such as 'my work has a hard physicality', recalls June in *The Player*). Ralph is convinced that Marian had a one night stand affair with a fellow artist three years earlier. At first denying everything, Marian eventually confesses ("I was drunk... It didn't mean anything... He didn't come in me"), though out of exasperation rather than guilt.

Lois Kaiser (Jennifer Jason Leigh), a skilled purveyor of telephone sex ('I can feel your balls against my ass'), and Jerry Kaiser (Chris Penn with a teutonic joke name), a swimming pool maintenance man. Jerry appears vaguely troubled by his wife's occupation, unable to accept that she regards it as simply a job, enabling her to work from home (with no worries about childcare) for good money. A confrontation with a lecherous ex-con at the jazz bar forces Lois to confront the sordid sexual demands (he offers her $200 for a blow job) she normally deals with over the safe distance of a telephone line. Altman seems to be making a point (not a very clear one) about the thin line between phone sex (fantasy) and prostitution (reality). Initially contemptuous of her would-be client, Lois appears to resent Jerry obliging the man to back off ('I could have used that money'), while Jerry is humiliated by the experience.

Honey Bush (Lili Taylor with a no-comment-needed name), daughter of Doreen Piggot, stepdaughter of Earl (who, she strongly hints, abused her as a child), and Bill Bush (Robert Downey Jr.), a trainee film make-up artist and rabid womaniser. Close friends of the Kaisers, Bill likes to keep Jerry closely informed of his numerous conquests, taking him along for the ride when possible. Asked to look after their neighbours' apartment while the latter are on holiday, the Bushs more or less take the place over, inviting Lois and Jerry round for a party. Curiously, this plotline shys away from the darker, more perverse tone of the Carver original (*Neighbors*), where Bill ends up trying on female underwear, a blouse ('burgundy') and a skirt ('black and white checks') left in the apartment.

Short Cuts – Andy Bitkower (Lyle Lovett) with the ill-fated cake

Gene Shepard (Tim Robbins), a bad tempered motorcycle cop and another womaniser, and Sherri Shepard (Madeleine Stowe), sister of Marian Wyman and one of her regular models. Gene hates the family dog, Suzy (a he), convinced that it is somehow aware of his adultery ('that fucking dog knows') and abandons it in the street one day. Tearful pressure from the three Shephard children obliges him to bring Suzy back again (having first cruised the streets on his bike in a prolonged search). Sherri spends much of her time talking with Marian on the phone, discussing her unsatisfactory sex life with Gene ('he won't do oral'). Her main source of entertainment is listening to Gene's ridiculous lies as he attempts to hide his affairs from her.

In addition, though no longer quite a family, there is Stormy Weathers (Peter Gallagher with a commented-on joke name), a cocky helicopter pilot, and Betty Weathers (Frances McDormand), his estranged wife and Gene Shepard's current lover (Gene makes a pass at Claire Kane after stopping her oddly adorned 'clown car' for 'driving too slow'). Betty has another, out of town affair going. Stormy registers his feelings about this by carving up his former wife's furniture with an electric saw and then hacking up her dresses with a pair of scissors.

Opening *Short Cuts* with a fleet of helicopters spraying anti-medfly insecticide over night-time Los Angeles (presumably a *M*A*S*H* or possibly *Whirlybirds* homage/injoke), Altman delivers a credits sequence as audacious and accomplished as the one which kicks off *The Player*. With whirring helicopter blades on the soundtrack (the machines are heard before they are seen), the production credits drift across and around the screen, as colourful and gaudy as neon signs, moving apart line by line only to flicker and disappear. The title, SHORT CUTS, appears as fragments which join together to form the two words. The camera, often mounted on a helicopter, glides over the city skyline, moving past and away from a briefly focused sign warning LA citizens of the medfly spraying. Altman's familiar 'eavesdropping' style, slow zooms and all, is at full strength. A pulsing drumbeat score takes over from the helicopter blades as we are introduced to the main characters, deftly intercut with the relentless helicopters (Altman wanted to give the characters two experiences in common: the pesticide spraying and, three hours on, a climactic/anticlimactic earthquake). Earl sits in his limousine, contemptuous of the two wealthy, drugged-out clients in the back. Howard and Ann sit at home watching the former discuss the medfly problem on his tv news editorial. Zoe plays at a concert, watched by the largely uninterested Stuart, Claire, Ralph and Marian. Without working out quite how, the Wymans find that they have invited the Kanes (whom they barely know) to dinner. Away from high culture, Jerry Kaiser checks over his boat (drydocked in the Kaiser's back gar-

Short Cuts – Lois Kaiser (Jennifer Jason Leigh) talks dirty

den) while Lois, with half an eye on Howard Finnigan's tv bulletin, satisfies another customer (Annie Ross/Tess Trainer takes over on soundtrack, singing 'Prisoner of Life', a pretty accurate theme song). Earl calls in at the diner to see Doreen, who bluntly points out that he is supposed to be working. At the jazz bar, with Tess in full flow, Honey and Bill discuss apartment minding with the soon-to-depart owners. As the helicopters finish their rounds, Gene and Sherri Shepard argue over the safety of the medfly killer (Gene's mood is not helped by the dog's continual barking), oblivious to Howard's televised explanation of the necessity for spraying.

Impressive as this opening sequence is, it creates problems for the rest of the film. The remaining two hours and forty five minutes do not live up to it, unreeling in a rather one-note fashion. Worse, the bulk of the film feels redundant. *Short Cuts* says what it has to say, articulating its characters, themes and style, in the first fifteen minutes (the time it would take to tell one short story). Tess's song, 'Prisoner of Life' lays out the central idea: 'Life's good. Life's bad' (mostly the latter). The unexpected events and accompanying uncertainties are what keep people going, drifting along without learning or maturing. Adultery, accidental death, suicide, murder and natural disaster are just extras in life's rich pageant. Nothing really changes.

In attempting to underline the 'authenticity' of his characters, Altman lapses into overkill. People urinate, scratch their behinds, squeeze blackheads, fart, wash their genitals, swear and shout a lot. Lois Kaiser 'talks dirty' to a client while changing one of her children's nappies ('Yeah baby'). To emphasize that Zoe Trainer (who, like Tess, has no equivalent in Carver's stories) is a little strange, Altman has her float (naked) in a swimming pool as if drowned, deliberately cut her hand on a drinking glass and play music till she expires in the fume filled garage (ten years after appearing as a kid from *Fame* (tv division), Lori Singer still plays a mean cello). Jack Lemmon is brought on (as Paul Finnigan, Howard's estranged father) to deliver a pointless, self-indulgent monologue explaining how he came to screw his wife's sister.

Altman also overplays his camera technique at times, as when he zooms in on the injured Casey's untouched glass of milk, then cuts and zooms out from the image of a spilled glass of milk playing on the Piggot's television (part of a safety commercial). Similarly, while Lois delivers her 'come on' lines ('grope my hot pink pussy') down the 'phone, the camera zooms in on Jerry looking just a little perturbed. This heavy-handed approach is symptomatic of the director's uncertainty as to how to tell so many stories at once (a problem which did not arise in *Nashville*), without losing his audience. The end result is that, contrary to his intentions, Altman reproduces the letter of Carver (albeit in mangled fashion), but little of the spirit. A comparison of two storylines with the Carver originals illustrates this failure.

The Finnigan's story, taken from *A Small, Good Thing*, is a typical example. While Casey lies prone in hospital, the baker commissioned to make his birthday cake phones the Finnigans to ask about collection and payment. A distraught Howard gives him short shrift, first telling him to get off the line, then, when called again, becoming abusive ('Fuck you asshole. Fuck you') and the baker, Andy Bitkower (Lyle Lovett), retaliates by making malicious phone calls throughout the night ('I wanna talk about that little bastard Casey'). In an unlikely twist, Bitkower cruelly plays on the boy's name and love of baseball by reciting lines from Ernest Lawrence Thayer's poem 'Casey at the Bat' ('Casey has struck out') to Ann Finnigan the night her son dies. When Ann and Howard angrily confront Bitkower over his behaviour (telling him that Casey is now dead), the baker repents in an understated fashion, persuading the distraught couple to sit down and eat some hot rolls ('a good thing at a time like this'). This is the most powerful moment in the film (impressively played by Andie MacDowell in particular), yet even here Altman coarsens Carver's work, using a sledgehammer instead of a gentle prod. Carver's baker is put out rather than malicious. There is no poetical taunting (the boy is called Scotty in the original).

Furthermore, he wants to explain why he behaved as he did ('what it comes down to is I don't know how to act anymore, it would seem'). In the film, the characters get caught up in the earthquake, dissipating the mood and effect of their particular narrative.

More disturbing is the reworking of *Tell the Women We're Going*, where a Bill and a Jerry pursue two uninterested teenage girls out for a bicycle ride in the country. Here it is Jerry who takes the lead, expressing his lust in violently misogynist terms ('You see the look that cunt gave me?'). In a savage blurring of sex and violence, Jerry kills both girls with a rock, while Bill looks on, dumbstruck. Not a pleasant story by any means, but a resonant account of psychotic, woman-hating aggression at work. In *Short Cuts*, Bill does his usual smooth-talking act, winning the girls' attention, only to have Jerry spoil the day by bludgeoning one of them to death (the implication being that Lois's work has corrupted his mind, triggering a misogynist rage). Like Bill, the audience has little opportunity to ponder this act, as it is immediately followed by the earthquake (the murdered girl is reported as the quake's only casualty). If Altman is playing with viewer responses to screen violence, especially violence against women (with blatant sexual connotations), his methods are dubious. In the fishing scenes, the naked corpse of the young rape/murder victim is almost entirely unblemished (and face-up in the water) as the repeated zoom-ins make clear. One of the fishermen (Buck Henry) takes pictures of the body (we are all voyeurs, after all), which, in a 'humorous' mix-up, get switched with pictures taken by Bill showing Honey wearing bloody make-up. 'Real' and fake violence collide, with Honey and the fisherman both unnerved by what they see. Only the audience knows what they are *really* seeing (would a photo processor develop pictures of a corpse without comment or query?). Some interesting points are raised here, but then, like so much in the film, nervously dropped with a jokey, throwaway tagline.

It is this lack of development or resolution (or even a point of view) that finally prevents *Short Cuts* from overcoming its misdirected (if laudable) scope and ambition (what use are twenty two characters when only a handful attract any interest, let alone sympathy?). The showdown between Ralph and Marian over the latter's alleged adultery typifies this failure. In a pre-dinner party stand-up shouting match, Marian admits first a kiss, then a grope, then full sex, her resentment at Ralph's questions ever rising (for unlikely reasons Marian is naked from the waist down, her pubic hair on full display). The mutual resentment continues over dinner, with snide remarks on both sides. Unlike the confessions of *Come Back to the Five and Dime, Jimmy Dean, Jimmy Dean*, Marian's admission brings no sense of relief, release or catharsis. Only alcoholic stupor produces any modicum of peace. If *Short Cuts* has any statement to make, it is that the best way through life is drunk, a philosophy expounded by Burt Reynolds 'buddy' movies nearly two decades earlier.

Released in the United States in October 1993, *Short Cuts* picked up some ecstatic reviews, being hailed as surefire Academy Award material. The film's earlier success at the Venice Film Festival (where, aside from the Best Film Award, the main cast jointly received the Best Acting Award) helped boost its prestige, with critics the world over hailing it as a masterpiece. This view was by no means unanimous, however, especially in *Short Cuts'* country of origin. New York writer James Wolcott dismissed the film as 'nothing but tricks... one smooth, knowing continuous sneer'. Many found it overlong, confusing, depressing and gratuitously violent. The old accusation of misogyny resurfaced (with, it must be said, some justification). The box-office returns proved disappointing as, unlike *The Player*, with its 'spot the star' gimmick, *Short Cuts* had no obvious appeal to mainstream audiences. Publicity lines such as 'From two American masters comes a movie like no other' failed to make much impact. The anticipated multiple Academy Award nominations, which would have boosted public interest in the film, didn't materialize. Altman had to be content with a rather token Best Director nomination, losing out on the night to Steven Spielberg and his Holocaust drama, *Schindler's List* (1993). Eventually written off as a commercial flop in America, *Short Cuts* fared much better in European territories, despite limited 'arthouse' distribution. Virtually all the leading critics loved it (in Britain at any rate) and, in this respect at least, Altman could congratulate himself on another personal triumph.

With *Short Cuts* a definite *succès d'estime*, Altman commenced work on his follow up production, the longstanding *Pret a Porter* (aka *Ready to Wear*) project. Dating back to the director's Paris sojourn in the mid-eighties, this script is a murder mystery (with no murder) set against the backdrop of the capital's bi-annual 'ready to wear' fashion show (enabling Altman to explore and satirize a particularly bizarre subculture). Altman's friendship with top fashion designer Sonia Rykiel gave him further insight into the workings of the business and access to the actual Spring show for authentic location filming, which commenced in March 1994, lasting over ten weeks. The cast line-up is impressive, with Lauren Bacall as the retired head of *American Vogue* magazine (allegedly based on Diane Vreeland), Sally Kellerman as Sissy Wanamaker, the editor of *Harper's Bazaar*, Marcello Mastroianni as Sergei, a 'mysterious Russian tailor' and Sophia Loren as Isabella de la Fontaine, the widow of the much-hated top man in fashion administration. Assorted designers, journalists, photographers and lookers-on are played by Kim Basinger, Lyle Lovett, Lili Taylor, Julia Roberts, Linda Hunt (Ma

Oxheart in *Popeye*), Tim Robbins and Anouk Aimée (presumably *At Lake Lugano* is forgiven/forgotten). Needless to say, many genuine high fashion celebrities make appearances as themselves. The absurd yet utterly straightfaced world of fashion shows is a gift of a subject for a director so adept at dissecting the concept of celebrity (and the artifice it leans on), and *Pret a Porter* is a respectable if hardly profound new work in the Altman canon.

Acting as his own (co)producer for the first time since *Secret Honor*, Altman co-wrote the script for *Pret a Porter* with Barbara Shulgasser. As expected, his production team included regulars Scott Bushnell, Steven Altman and Geraldine Peroni. The director of photography credit is shared by Pierre Mignot and Jean Lepine, the latter returning to the Altman fold after a one film break. Aside from his short stint on *Aria*, Mignot last worked with Altman on the ill-fated *Beyond Therapy*, a film which saw Paris locations used (and abused) in a less than impressive fashion. Thankfully, on this occasion script and setting are as compatible as could be wished.

Another large scale multi-character/multi-storyline 'tapestry', *Pret a Porter* kicks off the day before the opening of the Spring show, as various magazine editors, photographers, reporters and bootmakers arrive at the Charles de Gaulle airport in Paris. FAD–TV reporter Kitty Potter (Basinger) offers her thoughts on the various comings and goings (a typical Altman linking device). The 'murder' subplot is set in motion when, after a mysterious encounter with Sergei Oblomov, the head of the French fashion council chokes to death on a ham sandwich. As the fashion show commences, various mini-dramas ensue. One designer, Simone Lowenthal (Anouk Aimée), feels her new collection is doomed, as her heavily pregnant top model, Albertine (Ute Lemper), can't wear any of the clothes. Several magazine editors employ devious means in their attempts to lure top fashion photographer Milo O'Brannagan (Stephen Rea) away from *Vogue* magazine. Two male designers enjoy a secret affair, unaware that their respective partners are doing exactly the same thing. The final event of the show is the unveiling of Simone Lowenthal's new look. Her models stride onto the catwalk stark naked, led by the proudly pregnant Albertine.

A lightweight, slightly self-indulgent farce with a few mild satirical trimmings, *Pret a Porter* provides a certain amount of enjoyment without making too much effort to engage the brain. Altman's use of the real shows (filmed in fairly straight documentary style) gives the film moments of authenticity, though there is a case for arguing that these glimpses of the 'genuine' article sit a little uneasily with the unashamedly caricature characters and a tendency towards the surreal. Altman claims that he intended *Pret a Porter* as a 'celebration' of the fashion business, which sounds like a plea for leniency from both the audience and the various fashion designers who lent their talents to the production. Unlike *Short Cuts* (or *Health* or *A Wedding* or *Nashville*) there is no underlying 'message' (or anything much) lurking beneath the surface. Premiered at the Ziegfield Theatre, New York in December 1994, *Pret a Porter* met with a mixed reception, the overall opinion being that the film is a frenetic comedy which just happens to use the Paris fashion scene for background and decoration (and a nude finale). Kim Basinger and Sophia Loren were singled out for praise (the latter's demure striptease for former lover Marcello Mastroianni probably helped), while Lauren Bacall complained that her role had been drastically cut. *C'est la vie.*

Never one to pause for breath, Altman has a further project in preproduction, a film version of Tony Kushner's Broadway hit play *Angels in America*, an award-winning drama concerning the AIDS virus and its effect on a gay community. Like the play, the film will be in two parts, *Millennium Approaches* and *Perestroika*, shot simultaneously. There can be no doubt that Robert Altman intends to continue working for as long as possible. With his reputation and bankability secure, only his advancing years and somewhat fragile health can slow him down (fortunately, the years of serious drinking are long behind him). As Altman said in a recent interview, 'The only ending I know of is death'.

Appendix

Between 1977 and 1979, Altman acted as producer to *Welcome to LA* (1977), *The Late Show* (1977), *Remember My Name* (1978) and *Rich Kids* (1979), all financed and made through Lion's Gate. *Welcome to LA* and *Remember My Name* were both written and directed by Alan Rudolph, who'd previously worked for Altman as second assistant director on *California Split*, assistant director on *Nashville* and as co-writer for *Buffalo Bill and the Indians*. Altman claims to have had little involvement with the films, merely providing the finance, though *Welcome to LA* bears signs of his influence (oddball characters, multiple storylines, melancholy atmosphere). Rudolph has gone on to establish himself as an engagingly offbeat film-maker with films such as *Choose Me* (1984), *Trouble in Mind* (1985), *Made in Heaven* (1987), *The Moderns* (1988) and *Equinox* (1993).

The Late Show, a jokey homage to the private eye genre, marked a return to films for writer/director Robert Benton. Co-author of *Bonnie and Clyde*, Benton had made an acclaimed directorial debut with *Bad Company* (1972), a downbeat western, only to suffer a career slump. After his collaboration with Altman, Benton concentrated on safely mainstream films, enjoying major commercial success with *Kramer versus Kramer* (1979) and *Places in the Heart* (1984).

Rich Kids, a mildly interesting teenage drama, was a project developed by George W. George, Altman's co-producer/director on *The James Dean Story*. Robert M. Young (not to be confused with the British director, Robert Young) directed the film from a script by Judith Ross, George's wife. United Artists agreed to part finance *Rich Kids* on the condition that Altman would take over the direction if Young (primarily a documentary film-maker) ran into difficulties. Head of production Steven Bach felt that Altman's involvement made the film viable, despite the disappointing returns from *The Long Goodbye, Thieves Like Us* and *Buffalo Bill and the Indians*.

Produced on modest budgets (*Rich Kids*, for example, cost $2.5 million), *Welcome to LA, The Late Show, Remember My Name* and *Rich Kids* met with a fair amount of critical success but (like many of Altman's own films) only minimal distribution. Altman's career difficulties during the late seventies brought his work as a producer to an abrupt halt. Fourteen years on, he has resumed this former role, producing *Mrs Parker and The Vicious Circle* (1994), a biopic of the writer Dorothy Parker, for Alan Rudolph.

Filmography

The following list includes all of Altman's feature length films produced for the cinema. *The James Dean Story* and *Once Upon a Savage Night* (*Nightmare in Chicago*) are not included, as the former is a documentary and the latter a television play later re-edited for a brief theatrical run. All the films from *Countdown* onwards are in colour. Where a widescreen process was employed (usually Panavision), this has been noted. A few of Altman's films exist in more than one version. Both *Buffalo Bill and the Indians* and *Popeye* were cut by around twenty minutes for overseas release, while *Health* runs a few minutes longer in the version seen outside the United States. *That Cold Day in the Park* appears to have been hacked about several times by its distributor(s), resulting in at least three different running times.

CHRISTMAS EVE

(1947) United Artists

Co-writer (original story only). Uncredited.

THE BODYGUARD

(1948) RKO

Co-writer (original story only).

CORN'S A POPPIN

(1951) Crest

Co-writer.

THE DELINQUENTS

(1955, released 1957, 71 mins) United Artists

Producer: Robert Altman, *Screenplay*: Altman, *Photography*: Charles Paddock (black and white), *Art direction*: Chet Allen, *Editing*: Helene Turner, *Sound*: Bob Post, *Music*: Bill Nolan.

Cast: Tom Laughlin (Scotty), Peter Miller (Cholly), Richard Bakalyan (Eddy), Rosemary Howard (Janice), Helene Hawley (Mrs White), Leonard Belove (Mr White), Lotus Corelli (Mrs Wilson), James Lantz (Mr Wilson), Christine Altman (Sissy).

COUNTDOWN

(1968, 101 mins) Warner Brothers

Executive Producer: William Conrad, *Producer*: James Lydon, *Screenplay*:

Loring Mandel (based on the novel *The Pilgrim Project* by Hank Searls), *Photography*: William W. Spencer (Panavision), *Art Direction*: Jack Poplin, *Editing*: Gene Milford, *Sound*: Everett A. Hughes, *Music*: Leonard Rosenman.

Cast: James Caan (Lee Stegler), Robert Duvall (Chiz), Joanna Moore (Mickey), Barbara Baxley (Jean), Charles Aidman (Gus), Steve Ihnat (Ross), Michael Murphy (Rick), Bobby Riha Jr (Stevie).

THAT COLD DAY IN THE PARK

(1969, 106/110/115 mins) Factor-Altman-Mirell Films Ltd/Commonwealth International

Producers: Donald Factor, Leon Mirell, *Screenplay*: Gillian Freeman (based on the novel by Richard Miles), *Photography*: Laszlo Kovacs, *Art Direction*: Leon Ericksen, *Editing*: Danford B. Greene, *Sound*: John Guselle, *Music*: Johnny Mandel, *Associate Producer*: Robert Eggenweiler.

Cast: Sandy Dennis (Frances Austen), Michael Burns (Boy), Suzanne Benton (Nina), John Garfield Jr. (Nick), Luana Anders (Sylvia), Edward Greenhalgh (Dr Stevenson), Michael Murphy (The Rounder).

M°A°S°H

(1970, 116 mins) Twentieth Century Fox

Producer: Ingo Preminger, *Screenplay*: Ring Lardner Jr. (based on the novel by Richard Hooker), *Photography*: Harold E. Stine (Panavision), *Art Direction*: Jack Martin Smith, Arthur Lonergan and Leon Ericksen (credited as 'Associate Producer'), *Editing*: Danford B. Greene, *Sound*: Bernard Freericks, John Stack, *Music*: Johnny Mandel, *Special Effects*: L.B. Abbott, Art Cruickshank.

Cast: Donald Sutherland (Hawkeye Pierce), Elliott Gould (Trapper John McIntyre), Tom Skerritt (Duke Forrest),

Sally Kellerman (Margaret 'Hotlips' Houlihan), Robert Duvall (Frank Burns), Rene Auberjonois (Father Mulcahy), Jo Ann Pflug (Lt. Dish), Roger Bowen (Col. Blake), Gary Burghoff (Cpl. Radar O'Reilly), John Schuck (Painless Waldowski), Michael Murphy (Capt. Marston), Fred Williamson (Spearchucker Jones), Kim Atwood (Ho Jon), Bud Cort (Pvt. Boone), David Arkin (Sgt. Major Vollmer).

BREWSTER McCLOUD

(1970, 104 mins) Lion's Gate/Metro Goldwyn Mayer

Producer: Lou Adler, *Screenplay*: Doran William Cannon and (uncredited) Altman and Brian McKay, *Photography*: Jordan Cronenweth, Lamar Boren (Panavision), *Art Direction*: George W. Davis, Preston Ames, *Editing*: Lou Lombardo, *Sound*: Harry W. Tetrick, William McCaughey, *Music*: Gene Page, *Special Effects* (wing design): Leon Ericksen, *Associate Producers*: Robert Eggenweiler, James Margellos, *Assistant Director*: Tommy Thompson.

Cast: Bud Cort (Brewster McCloud), Sally Kellerman (Louise), Michael Murphy (Frank Shaft), William Windom (Haskell Weeks), Shelley Duvall (Suzanne), Rene Auberjonois (Lecturer), Stacy Keach (Abraham Wright), Margaret Hamilton (Daphne Heap), John Schuck (Johnson), Jennifer Salt (Hope), Bert Remsen (Douglas Breen).

McCABE AND MRS MILLER

(1971, 121 mins) Warner Brothers

Producers: David Foster, Mitchell Brower, *Screenplay*: Altman, Brian McKay (based on the novel *McCabe* by Edmund Naughton), *Photography*: Vilmos Zsigmond (Panavision), *Art Direction*: Leon Ericksen, *Editing*: Lou Lombardo, *Sound*: John Gusselle, William A. Thompson, *Music*: Leonard Cohen, *Costumes*: Ilse Richter,

Special Effects: Marcel Vercoutere, *Associate Producer*: Robert Eggenweiler, *Assistant Director*: Tommy Thompson.

Cast: Warren Beatty (John McCabe), Julie Christie (Constance Miller), Rene Auberjonois (Patrick Sheehan), Hugh Millais (Dog Butler), Shelley Duvall (Ida Coyl), Michael Murphy (Eugene Sears), John Schuck (Smalley), Corey Fischer (Preacher), William Devane (Clement Samuels), Anthony Holland (Ernie Hollander), Bert Remsen (Bart Coyl), Keith Carradine (Cowboy), Jace Vander Veen (Breed), Manfred Schulz (Kid), Bob Fortier (Town Drunk).

IMAGES

(1972, 101 mins) Lion's Gate/Hemdale/Columbia

Producer: Tommy Thompson, *Screenplay*: Altman (extracts from *In Search of Unicorns* by Susannah York), *Photography*: Vilmos Zsigmond (Panavision), *Art Direction*: Leon Ericksen, *Editing*: Graeme Clifford, *Sound*: Liam Saurin, Rodney Holland, *Music*: John Williams, Stomu Yamash'ta (special sounds), *Costumes*: Jack Gallagher.

Cast: Susannah York (Cathryn), Rene Auberjonois (Hugh), Marcel Bozzuffi (Rene), Hugh Millais (Marcel), Cathryn Harrison (Susannah), John Morley (Neighbour).

THE LONG GOODBYE

(1973, 111 mins) Lion's Gate/United Artists

Executive Producer: Elliott Kastner, *Producer*: Jerry Bick, *Screenplay*: Leigh Brackett (based on the novel by Raymond Chandler), *Photography*: Vilmos Zsigmond (Panavision), *Editing*: Lou Lombardo, *Sound*: John V. Speak, *Music*: John Williams, *Costumes*: Kent James, Marjorie Wahl, *Associate Producer*: Robert Eggenweiler, *Assistant Director*: Tommy Thompson.

Cast: Elliott Gould (Philip Marlowe), Nina Van Pallandt (Eileen Wade), Sterling Hayden (Roger Wade), Mark Rydell (Marty Augustine), Henry Gibson (Dr Verringer), David Arkin (Harry), Jim Bouton (Terry Lennox), Warren Berlinger (Morgan), Jo Ann Brody (Jo Ann Eggenweiler), David Carradine (Prisoner), Arnold Schwarzenegger (Heavy).

THIEVES LIKE US

(1974, 123 mins) United Artists

Executive Producer: George Litto, *Producer*: Jerry Bick, *Screenplay*: Calder Willingham, Joan Tewkesbury, Altman (based on the novel by Edward Anderson), *Photography*: Jean Boffety, *Editing*: Lou Lombardo, *Sound*: Don Matthews, *Visual Consultant*: Jack DeGovia, *Associate Producers*: Robert Eggenweiler, Thomas Hal Phillips, *Assistant Director*: Tommy Thompson.

Cast: Keith Carradine (Bowie), Shelley Duvall (Keechie), John Schuck (Chicamaw Mobley), Bert Remsen (T-Dub Masefield), Louise Fletcher (Mattie), Tom Skerritt (Dee Mobley), Al Scott (Captain Stammers), John Roper (Jasbo), Mary Waits (Noel Joy), Rodney Lee Jr. (James Mattingly), William Watters (Alvin), Joan Tewkesbury (Lady in train station).

CALIFORNIA SPLIT

(1974, 109 mins) Columbia

Executive Producers: Aaron Spelling, Leonard Goldberg, *Producers*: Joseph Walsh, Altman, *Screenplay*: Joseph Walsh, *Photography*: Paul Lohmann (Panavision), *Art Direction*: Leon Ericksen, *Editing*: Lou Lombardo, *Sound*: Jim Webb, Kay Rose, *Music*: Phyllis Shotwell, *Associate Producer*: Robert Eggenweiler, *Assistant Director*: Tommy Thompson.

Cast: George Segal (Bill Denny), Elliott Gould (Charlie Waters), Ann Prentiss (Barbara Miller), Gwen Welles (Susan Peters), Joseph Walsh (Sparkie), Edward

Walsh (Lew), Bert Remsen (Helen Brown), Barbara Ruick (Reno Barmaid), Jeff Goldblum (Lloyd Harris), John Considine (Man at bar).

NASHVILLE

(1975, 159 mins) ABC/Paramount

Executive Producers: Martin Starger, Jerry Weintraub, *Producer*: Altman, *Screenplay*: Joan Tewkesbury, *Photography*: Paul Lohmann (Panavision), *Editing*: Sidney Levin, Dennis Hill, *Sound*: Jim Webb, Chris McLaughlin, *Music Arranger*: Richard Baskin, *Associate Producers*: Robert Eggenweiler, Scott Bushnell, *Assistant Directors*: Tommy Thompson, Alan Rudolph.

Cast: David Arkin (Norman), Barbara Baxley (Lady Pearl), Ned Beatty (Delbert Reese), Karen Black (Connie White), Ronee Blakley (Barbara Jean), Timothy Brown (Tommy Brown), Keith Carradine (Tom Frank), Geraldine Chaplin (Opal), Robert Doqui (Wade), Shelley Duvall (LA Joan), Allen Garfield (Barnett), Henry Gibson (Haven Hamilton), Scott Glenn (Glenn Kelly), Jeff Goldblum (Tricycle Man), Barbara Harris (Albuquerque), David Hayward (Kenny Fraiser), Michael Murphy (John Triplette), Allan Nicholls (Bill), Dave Peel (Bud Hamilton), Christina Raines (Mary), Bert Remsen (Star), Lily Tomlin (Linnea Reese), Gwen Welles (Sueleen Gay), Keenan Wynn (Mr Green), Elliott Gould (himself), Julie Christie (herself).

BUFFALO BILL AND THE INDIANS, OR SITTING BULL'S HISTORY LESSON

(1976, 123 mins (US), 104 mins (GB)) Lion's Gate/Dino De Laurentiis/United Artists

Executive Producer: David Susskind, *Producer*: Altman, *Screenplay*: Alan Rudolph, Altman (based on the play *Indians* by Arthur Kopit), *Photography*: Paul Lohmann (Panavision), *Production*

Design: Tony Masters, *Editing*: Peter Appleton, Dennis Hill, *Sound*: Jim Webb, Chris McLaughlin, *Music*: Richard Baskin, *Costumes*: Anthony Powell, *Associate Producers*: Robert Eggenweiler, Scott Bushnell, Jack Cashin, *Assistant Director*: Tommy Thompson.

Cast: Paul Newman ('Buffalo' Bill Cody, the Star), Burt Lancaster (Ned Buntline, the Legendmaker), Harvey Keitel (the Relative), Geraldine Chaplin (Annie Oakley, the Sureshot), John Considine (the Sureshot's Manager), Frank Kaquitts (Sitting Bull, the Indian), Will Sampson (Interpreter), Joel Grey (the Producer), Kevin McCarthy (the Publicist), Allan Nicholls (the Journalist), Denver Pyle (the Indian Agent), Pat McCormick (the President), Shelley Duvall (the First Lady), Bert Remsen (Bartender).

THREE WOMEN

(1977, 123 mins) Lion's Gate/ Twentieth Century Fox

Producer: Altman, *Screenplay*: Altman, *Photography*: Charles Rosher (Panavision), *Art Direction*: James D. Vance, *Editing*: Dennis Hill, *Sound*: Jim Webb, Chris McLaughlin, *Music*: Gerald Busby, *Murals*: Bodhi Wind, *Associate Producers*: Robert Eggenweiler, Scott Bushnell, *Assistant Director*: Tommy Thompson.

Cast: Shelley Duvall (Millie Lammoreaux), Sissy Spacek (Mildred 'Pinky' Rose), Janice Rule (Willie Hart), Bob Fortier (Edgar Hart), John Cromwell (Mr Rose), Ruth Nelson (Mrs Rose), Belita Moreno (Alcira), Craig Richard Nelson (Dr Maas), Beverly Ross (Deidre), John Davey (Dr Norton).

A WEDDING

(1978, 125 mins) Lion's Gate/ Twentieth Century Fox

Executive Producer: Tommy Thompson, *Producer*: Altman, *Screenplay*: John Considine, Patricia Resnick, Allan Nicholls,

Altman, *Photography*: Charles Rosher, *Editing*: Tony Lombardo, *Sound*: Jim Webb, Chris McLaughlin, Jim Bourgeois, Jim Steube, *Fanfare music*: John Hotchkis, *Music Director*: Tom Walls, *Associate Producers*: Robert Eggenweiler, Scott Bushnell, *Assistant Director*: Tommy Thompson.

Cast: Lillian Gish (Nettie Sloan), Ruth Nelson (Beatrice Sloan Cory), Desi Arnaz Jr. (Dino Corelli), Vittorio Gassman (Luigi Corelli), Nina Van Pallandt (Regina Corelli), Belita Moreno (Daphne Corelli), Dina Merrill (Antoinette Sloan Goddard), Pat McCormick (Mackenzie Goddard), Ann Ryerson (Victoria Cory), Carol Burnett (Tulip Brenner), Paul Dooley (Snooks Brenner), Amy Stryker (Muffin Brenner), Mia Farrow (Buffy Brenner), Dennis Christopher (Hughie Brenner), Cedric Scott (Randolph), Bob Fortier (Jim Habor), Geraldine Chaplin (Rita Billingsley), Lauren Hutton (Flo Farmer), Allan Nicholls (Jake Jacobs), John Considine (Jeff Kuykendall), Patricia Resnick (Redford), Howard Duff (Dr Jules Meecham), John Cromwell (Bishop Martin), Bert Remsen (William Williamson), Pam Dawber (Tracy Parrell), Gavan O'Hirlihy (Wilson Briggs), Marta Heflin (Shelby Munker), Beverly Ross (Nurse Janet Schulman), Craig Richard Nelson (Captain Reedley Roots).

QUINTET

(1979, 118 mins) Lion's Gate/ Twentieth Century Fox

Producer: Altman, *Screenplay*: Frank Barhydt, Patricia Resnick, Altman (based on a treatment by Lionel Chetwynd), *Photography*: Jean Boffety, *Production Design*: Leon Ericksen, *Art Direction*: Wolf Kroeger, *Editing*: Dennis Hill, *Sound*: Robert Gravenor, *Music*: Tom Pierson, *Costume Designer*: Scott Bushnell, *Assistant Director*: Tommy Thompson.

Cast: Paul Newman (Essex), Fernando Rey (Grigor), Bibi Andersson (Ambrosia),

Vittorio Gassman (St Christopher), Nina Van Pallandt (Deuca), Brigitte Fossey (Vivia), David Langton (Goldstar), Craig Richard Nelson (Redstone).

A PERFECT COUPLE

(1979, 111 mins) Lion's Gate/ Twentieth Century Fox

Executive Producer: Tommy Thompson, *Producer*: Altman, *Screenplay*: Allan Nicholls, Altman, *Photography*: Edmond L. Koons, *Production Design*: Leon Ericksen, *Editing*: Tony Lombardo, *Sound*: Robert Gravenor, Don Merritt, *Music*: Tony Berg, Allan Nicholls, Tom Pierson, *Associate Producers*: Robert Eggenweiler, Scott Bushnell, *Assistant Director*: Tommy Thompson.

Cast: Paul Dooley (Alex Theodopoulos), Marta Heflin (Sheila Shea), Titos Vandis (Panos Theodopoulos), Belita Moreno (Eleousa), Henry Gibson (Fred Bott), Dimitra Arliss (Athena), Allan Nicholls (Dana 115), Ann Ryerson (Sky 147), Dennis Franz (Costa), Ted Neeley (Teddy).

HEALTH aka H.E.A.L.T.H.

(1980, 96 mins (US), 100 mins (GB)) Lion's Gate/Twentieth Century Fox

Executive Producer: Tommy Thompson, *Producer*: Altman, *Screenplay*: Frank Barhydt, Paul Dooley, Altman, *Photography*: Edmond L. Koons, *Art Direction*: Robert Quinn, *Editing*: Tony Lombardo, Dennis Hill, Tom Benko, *Sound*: Robert Gravenor, Don Merritt, *Music*: Joseph Byrd, *Associate Producers*: Robert Eggenweiler, Scott Bushnell, *Assistant Director*: Tommy Thompson.

Cast: Lauren Bacall (Esther Brill), Glenda Jackson (Isabella Garnell), James Garner (Harry Wolff), Carol Burnett (Gloria Burbank), Paul Dooley (Dr Gill Gainey), Henry Gibson (Bobby Hammer), Donald Moffat (Colonel Cody/Lester Brill), Diane Stilwell (Willow Wertz), Alfre Woodard

(Sally Benbow), Ann Ryerson (Dr Ruth Ann Jackle), Bob Fortier (Security Chief), Allan Nicholls (Jake Jacobs), MacIntyre Dixon (Fred Munson), Dick Cavett (himself).

POPEYE

(1980, 114 mins (US), 95 mins (GB)) Paramount/Walt Disney

Producer: Robert Evans, *Screenplay*: Jules Feiffer (based on characters created by E.C. Segar), *Photography*: Giuseppe Rotunno (Technovision), *Production Designer*: Wolf Kroeger, *Editing*: Tony Lombardo, John W. Holmes, David Simmons, *Sound*: Robert Gravenor, Sam Gemette, *Music and Lyrics*: Harry Nilsson, *Additional score*: Tom Pierson, *Costumes*: Scott Bushnell, *Associate Producer*: Scott Bushnell.

Cast: Robin Williams (Popeye), Shelley Duvall (Olive Oyl), Ray Walston (Poopdeck Pappy), Paul Dooley (Wimpy), Paul Smith (Bluto), Richard Libertini (Geezil), Wesley Ivan Hurt (Swee'pea), Roberta Maxwell (Nana Oyl), MacIntyre Dixon (Cole Oyl), Donovan Scott (Castor Oyl), Donald Moffat (Taxman), Peter Bray (Oxblood Oxheart), Linda Hunt (Ma Oxheart), Allan Nicholls (Rough House), Bob Fortier (Bill Barnacle), David Arkin (Mailman), Dennis Franz (Spike).

COME BACK TO THE FIVE AND DIME, JIMMY DEAN, JIMMY DEAN

(1982, 102 mins) Sandcastle 5/Mark Goodson/Viacom

Executive Producer: Giraud Chester, *Producer*: Scott Bushnell, *Screenplay*: Ed Graczyk (based on his play), *Photography*: Pierre Mignot, *Production Design*: David Cropman, *Editing*: Jason Rosenfield, *Sound*: Richard Fitzgerald, *Music*: Allan Nicholls, *Costumes*: Scott Bushnell.

Cast: Sandy Dennis (Mona), Cher (Sissy), Karen Black (Joanne), Sudie Bond (Juanita), Marta Heflin (Edna Louise),

Kathy Bates (Stella Mae), Mark Patton (Joe).

STREAMERS

(1983, 118 mins) Mileti Productions/ United Artists Classics

Executive Producers: Robert Michael Geiser, John Roberdeau, *Producers*: Nick J. Mileti, Altman, *Screenplay*: David Rabe (based on his play), *Photography*: Pierre Mignot, *Art Direction*: Steven Altman, *Set Design*: Wolf Kroeger, *Editing*: Norman C. Smith, *Costumes*: Scott Bushnell, *Assistant Director*: Allan Nicholls.

Cast: Matthew Modine (Billy), Michael Wright (Carlyle), David Alan Grier (Roger), Mitchell Lichtenstein (Richie), Guy Boyd (Rooney), George Dzundza (Cokes), Albert Macklin (Martin).

O.C. AND STIGGS

(1983 (released 1987), 109 mins) Metro Goldwyn Mayer/United Artists

Executive Producer: Lewis Allen, *Producers*: Peter Newman, Altman, *Screenplay*: Donald Cantrell, Ted Mann (based on a short story, *The Ugly, Monstrous, Mindroasting Summer of O.C. and Stiggs* by Mann and Tod Carroll), *Photography*: Pierre Mignot, *Production Design*: Scott Bushnell, *Art Director*: David Cropman, *Editing*: Elizabeth Kling, *Music*: King Sunny Adé and his African Beats, *Associate Producer*: Scott Bushnell.

Cast: Daniel H. Jenkins (Oliver Cromwell Ogilvy), Neill Barry (Mark Stiggs), Paul Dooley (Randall Schwab), Jane Curtin (Elinore Schwab), Jon Cryer (Randall Schwab Jr.), Laura Urstein (Lenora Schwab), Victor Ho (Frank Tang), Ray Walston (Gramps), Martin Mull (Pat Coletti), Dennis Hopper (Sponson), Melvin Van Peebles (Wino Bob), Cynthia Nixon (Michelle), Louis Nye (Garth Sloan), Tina Louise (Florence Beaugereaux), Donald May (Jack Stiggs), Carla Borelli (Stella Stiggs).

SECRET HONOR

(1984, 85 mins) Sandcastle 5

Executive Producer: Scott Bushnell, *Producer*: Altman, *Associate Director*: Robert Harders, *Screenplay*: Donald Freed, Arnold M. Stone (based on their play), *Photography*: Pierre Mignot, *Art Direction*: Steven Altman, *Editing*: Juliet Weber, *Sound*: Bernard Hajdenberg, *Music*: George Burt, *Assistant Director*: Allan Nicholls.

Cast: Philip Baker Hall (Richard Nixon).

FOOL FOR LOVE

(1985, 107 mins) Cannon Films

Producers: Menahem Golan, Yoram Globus, *Screenplay*: Sam Shepard (based on his play), *Photography*: Pierre Mignot, *Production Design*: Steven Altman, *Editing*: Luce Grunenwaldt, Steve Dunn, *Sound*: Catherine D'Hoir, *Music*: George Burt, *Associate Producers:* Scott Bushnell, Mati Raz.

Cast: Sam Shepard (Eddie), Kim Basinger (May), Harry Dean Stanton (Old man), Randy Quaid (Martin), Martha Crawford (May's mother), Louise Egolf (Eddie's mother), Sura Cox (teenage May), Jonathan Skinner (teenage Eddie), April Russell (young May), Deborah McNaughton (the Countess), Lon Hill (Mr Valdes).

BEYOND THERAPY

(1987, 93 mins) Sandcastle Five/Roger Berlind/New World Pictures

Executive Producer: Roger Berlind, *Producer*: Steven M. Haft, *Screenplay*: Christopher Durang, Altman (based on Durang's play), *Photography*: Pierre Mignot, *Production Design*: Steven Altman, *Editing*: Steve Dunn, *Sound*: Francoise Coispeau, *Music*: Gabriel Yared, *Associate Producer*: Scott Bushnell.

Cast: Julie Hagerty (Prudence), Jeff Goldblum (Bruce), Glenda Jackson (Charlotte), Tom Conti (Stuart), Christopher Guest (Bob), Genevieve Page (Zizi), Cris Campion (Andrew), Sandrine Dumas (Cindy), Bertrand Bonvoisin (Le Gerant), Nicole Evans (cashier), Louis-Marie Taillefer (chef), Matthew Lesniak (Mr Bean), Laure Killing (Charlie).

ARIA

(1988) Lightyear Entertainment/Virgin Vision/Miramax Films. *Les Boréades* segment only.

VINCENT AND THEO

(1990, 138 mins) Belbo Films/Central Films/La Sept/Telepool/Rai Uno/Vara/Sofica-Valor/Arena Films

Executive Producer: David Conroy, *Producer*: Ludi Boeken, *Screenplay*: Julian Mitchell, *Photography*: Jean Lepine, *Production Design*: Steven Altman, *Editing*: Francoise Coispeau, Geraldine Peroni, *Sound*: Alain Curvelier, *Music*: Gabriel Yared, *Costumes*: Scott Bushnell, *Reproductions*: Robin Thiodet.

Cast: Tim Roth (Vincent Van Gogh), Paul Rhys (Theo Van Gogh), Johanna Ter Steege (Jo Bonger), Jean-Pierre Cassel (Dr Paul Gachet), Bernadette Giraud (Marguerite Gachet), Wladimir Yordanoff (Paul Gauguin), Adrian Brine (Uncle Cent), Jean-Francois Perrier (Leon Boussod), Hans Kesting (Andries Bonger), Jip Wijngaarden (Sien Hoornik), Anne Canovas (Marie).

THE PLAYER

(1992, 124 mins) Avenue Entertainment/Spelling Films International

Executive Producer: Cary Brokaw, *Producers*: David Brown, Michael Tolkin, Nick Wechsler, *Co-producer*: Scott Bushnell, *Screenplay*: Tolkin (based on his novel), *Photography*: Jean Lepine, *Production Design*: Steven Altman, *Editing*: Maysie Hoy, Geraldine Peroni, *Sound*: Michael Redbourn, *Music*: Thomas

Newman, *Assistant Directors*: Allan
Nicholls, C.C. Barnes.

Cast: Tim Robbins (Griffin Mill), Greta
Scacchi (June Gudmundsdottir), Fred
Ward (Walter Stuckel), Whoopi Goldberg
(Detective Susan Avery), Peter Gallagher
(Larry Levy), Brion James (Joel Levison),
Cynthia Stevenson (Bonnie Sherow),
Vincent D'Onofrio (David Kahane), Dean
Stockwell (Andy Civella), Richard E. Grant
(Tom Oakley), Sydney Pollack (Dick
Mellen), Lyle Lovett (Detective
DeLongpre), Dina Merrill (Celia), Frank
Barhydt (Frank Murphy), Michael Tolkin
(Eric Schecter), Stephen Tolkin (Carl
Schecter), Jeremy Piven (Steve Reeves),
Steve Allen, Richard Anderson, Rene
Auberjonois, Harry Belafonte, Shari
Belafonte, Karen Black, Michael Bowen,
Gary Busey, Robert Carradine, Charles
Champlin, Cher, James Coburn, Cathy Lee
Crosby, John Cusack, Brad Davis, Paul
Dooley, Thereza Ellis, Peter Falk, Felicia
Farr, Kasia Figura, Louise Fletcher,
Dennis Franz, Teri Garr, Leeza Gibbons,
Scott Glenn, Jeff Goldblum, Elliott Gould,
Joel Grey, David Alan Grier, Buck Henry,
Angelica Huston, Kathy Ireland, Steve
James, Maxine John-James, Sally
Kellerman, Sally Kirkland, Jack Lemmon,
Marlee Matlin, Andie MacDowell,
Malcolm McDowell, Jayne Meadows,
Martin Mull, Jennifer Nash, Nick Nolte,
Alexandra Powers, Bert Remsen, Guy
Remsen, Patricia Resnick, Burt Reynolds,
Jack Riley, Julia Roberts, Mimi Rogers,
Annie Ross, Alan Rudolph, Jill St John,
Susan Sarandon, Adam Simon, Rod
Steiger, Joan Tewkesbury, Brian Tochi,
Lily Tomlin, Robert Wagner, Ray Walston,
Bruce Willis, Marvin Young (themselves).

SHORT CUTS

**(1993, 188 mins) Fine Line Features/
Avenue Pictures/Spelling Films
International**

Executive Producer: Scott Bushnell,
Producer: Carey Brocaw, *Screenplay:*
Altman, Frank Barhydt (based on nine
short stories and a poem by Raymond
Carver: *Neighbors*; *They're Not Your
Husband*; *Vitamins*; *Will You Please Be
Quiet, Please?*; *So Much Water So Close to
Home*; *A Small, Good Thing*; *Jerry and
Molly and Sam*; *Collectors*; *Tell the Women
We're Going* and *Lemonade*), *Photography:*
Walt Lloyd (Panavision), *Production
design:* Steven Altman, *Editing:* Geraldine
Peroni, Suzy Elmiger, *Sound:* Eliza Paley,
Music: Mark Isham, *Associate Producers:*
Mike Kaplan, David Levy, *Assistant
Directors:* Allan Nicholls, Jeff Rafner.

Cast: Andie MacDowell (Ann Finnigan),
Bruce Davison (Howard Finnigan), Jack
Lemmon (Paul Finnigan), Zane Cassidy
(Casey Finnigan), Julianne Moore (Marian
Wyman), Matthew Modine (Ralph
Wyman), Anne Archer (Claire Kane), Fred
Ward (Stuart Kane), Jennifer Jason Leigh
(Lois Kaiser), Chris Penn (Jerry Kaiser),
Lili Taylor (Honey Bush), Robert Downey
Jr. (Bill Bush), Madeleine Stowe (Sherri
Shepard), Tim Robbins (Gene Shepard),
Lily Tomlin (Doreen Piggot), Tom Waits
(Earl Piggot), Frances McDormand (Betty
Weathers), Peter Gallagher (Stormy
Weathers), Annie Ross (Tess Trainer), Lori
Singer (Zoe Trainer), Lyle Lovett (Andy
Bitkower), Buck Henry (Gordon Johnson),
Huey Lewis (Vern Miller), Margery Bond
(Dora Willis), Robert Doqui (Knute Willis).

Videography

UNITED KINGDOM (PAL FORMAT)

While this guide to video availability will inevitably become out of date (though, considering the scant number of Altman releases in recent years, this may take a while), it seems useful to list the titles which can be obtained. All are taken from the prints released to British cinemas, so both *Buffalo Bill and the Indians* and *Popeye* remain viewable only in the edited versions. In most cases, the films shot in the scope format lose around half of the original screen picture in the transfer from celluloid to tape (the same 'pan and scan' process normally used for television screenings).

The following Robert Altman films are currently available on video in the United Kingdom:

M°A°S°H (CBS/FOX) (also available in widescreen)

McCABE AND MRS MILLER (Tartan) (widescreen – original Panavision format, also available on laserdisc)

BUFFALO BILL AND THE INDIANS (Braveworld/Spotlight) (widescreen)

COME BACK TO THE FIVE AND DIME, JIMMY DEAN, JIMMY DEAN (Braveworld/Spotlight)

STREAMERS (Arrow)

SECRET HONOR (Castle Hendring)

VINCENT AND THEO (Island World)

THE PLAYER (Guild) (also available on Pioneer laserdisc in widescreen)

SHORT CUTS (Artificial Eye/Fox Video) (rental version in pan and scan format, sell-through version in widescreen)

A number of Altman films have previously been released as rental tapes, but are now deleted from their distributors' catalogues. These include *Countdown* (Warner), *Brewster McCloud* (MGM/UA), *Images* (VCL), *The Long Goodbye* (Warner), *A Wedding* (CBS/Fox), *Quintet* (CBS/Fox), *Popeye* (Disney, both rental and retail), *O.C. & Stiggs* (MGM/UA), *Fool For Love* (Rank) and *Beyond Therapy* (New World). Some of these may still be found in video libraries and there are dealers who specialize in locating copies of deleted titles at reasonable prices (check the classified ad sections of film and video magazines, bearing in mind that any tape sold within the UK must have a certificate from the British Board of Film Classification).

UNITED STATES (NTSC FORMAT)

American video releases tend to go in and out of circulation more rapidly than their British counterparts. This list is, as far as possible, accurate to the beginning of 1995:

COUNTDOWN

THAT COLD DAY IN THE PARK (106 minute version)

M°A°S°H (also available on laserdisc)

BREWSTER McCLOUD (also available on laserdisc)

McCABE AND MRS MILLER (also available on laserdisc)

THE LONG GOODBYE (also available on laserdisc)

NASHVILLE

BUFFALO BILL AND THE INDIANS

A WEDDING

QUINTET

POPEYE (also available on laserdisc in pan and scan format)

COME BACK TO THE FIVE AND DIME, JIMMY DEAN, JIMMY DEAN

STREAMERS

O.C. AND STIGGS

SECRET HONOR

FOOL FOR LOVE

BEYOND THERAPY

VINCENT AND THEO (also available on laserdisc)

THE PLAYER (also available on laserdisc)

SHORT CUTS (also available on laserdisc)

Films on laserdisc are usually presented in their original cinema ratio. The growing popularity of this format in the United States means that there is less demand from film enthusiasts for widescreen video versions. Thus, tape releases are invariably in the more popular pan and scan format.

Bibliography

ANDREW, GEOFF, *The Films of Nicholas Ray*, Charles Letts & Co Ltd, London, 1991.

BACH, STEVEN, *Final Cut*, Faber & Faber, London, 1986.

BETROCK, ALAN, *I was a Teenage Juvenile Delinquent Rock 'n' Roll Beach Party Movie Book – A Complete Guide to the Teen Exploitation Film: 1954–1969*, Plexus, London, 1986.

FULLER, GRAHAM (ed), *Altman on Altman*, from *Projections 2*, ed John Boorman and Walter Donohue, Faber & Faber, London, 1993.

HALLIWELL, LESLIE, *Halliwell's Film Guide* (seventh edition), Grafton Books, London, 1989.

HALLIWELL, LESLIE, *Halliwell's Filmgoer's Companion* (ninth edition), Paladin, London, 1989.

HOGAN, DAVID J., *Who's Who of the Horrors and Other Fantasy Films*, A.S. Barnes & Company, Inc., New York, 1980.

KATZ, EPHRAIM, *The International Film Encyclopedia*, Macmillan, London, 1980.

KEYSSAR, HELEN, *Robert Altman's America*, Oxford University Press, New York, 1991.

KOLKER, ROBERT PHILLIP, *A Cinema of Loneliness* (second edition), Oxford University Press, New York, 1988.

MAST, GERALD, *A Short History of the Movies* (second edition), Bobbs-Merrill, Indiana, 1976.

MCGILLIGAN, PATRICK, *Robert Altman Jumping Off the Cliff*, St Martin's Press, New York, 1989.

NEWMAN, KIM, *Nightmare Movies*, Harmony Books, New York, 1988.

NICHOLLS, PETER, *Fantastic Cinema: An Illustrated Survey*, Ebury Press, London, 1984.

PEARY, DANNY, *A Guide for the Film Fanatic*, Simon & Schuster, Inc., New York, 1986.

Index

People

Bold type refers to illustrations.

Titles

(film unless otherwise stated).
Bold type refers to illustrations.